RUNNING REMOTE

LIAM MARTIN
AND ROB RAWSON

RUNNING REMOTE

MASTER THE LESSONS FROM THE WORLD'S MOST SUCCESSFUL REMOTE-WORK PIONEERS

HarperCollins Leadership
An Imprint of HarperCollins

Published by HarperCollins Leadership, an imprint of HarperCollins Focus LLC.

ISBN 978-1-4002-3215-4 (eBook)
ISBN 978-1-4002-3214-7 (HC)

Library of Congress Control Number: 2022936276

ISBN 978-1-4002-3932-0 (International edition)

Printed in Australia

To Daniel for helping us make this book a reality.

To Marielle and Marina, who have been such a massive support throughout this book and our lives.

And to Fahim, who inspires us to continue to work on helping the world transition to remote work.

CONTENTS

INTRO

The Async Mindset, the Async Method

Ever wonder what it would be like to live through a real revolution?

We're talking about a historic upheaval where old boundaries are destroyed, whole lifestyles and industries are overturned, and most of all, a new mindset is born, one that makes the recent past seem utterly, hopelessly archaic.

Well, you're in one—and it's bigger than you think. The far-reaching implications that our epoch will ultimately have on the thing we call work—what it's for, how it's done, what it feels like—are nothing short of the biggest change to our lives since the advent of electricity.

Here is the kicker—it isn't just about working remotely.

True, it's no secret that the world has gone remote in the steepest, fastest, most disruptive way imaginable. In the wake of humankind's first global pandemic since the invention of the computer, a giant portion of the working world flipped to remote with lightning speed, as one corporate giant after another announced that they're going all-remote, going hybrid, or offering sustainable remote options. In fact, even many sizable entities that grew and thrived in the traditional on-premise model—Dropbox, Microsoft, Apple, and so many others—have ultimately embraced permanent work-from-home, and many of them will never open an office again.

The fact that these changes are rapid and sweeping is obvious. What hasn't been as well understood is just how radical is this shift in mindset.

Where and when people work are not even half the story.

That's why this book isn't merely about remote work. It's about a whole new way that any company can work. It unveils a philosophy and methodology first discovered and developed by organizations well before COVID-19 hit. These organizations were the first to embrace the remote challenge. The question these frontrunners posed was simple: What if you could work with people all over the world, but you could never meet with anyone in person?

The answers they uncovered were groundbreaking, counterintuitive, and will likely transform the way we work—that is, the way everyone works—for all time.

THAT SINGLE LIMITATION—little to no in-person engagement—forced these remote-work pioneers to develop what we call the Async Mindset, relying on precise communication, highly developed processes, and irrefutable metrics. Put together, doing things the async way yields a surprising number of benefits, including hyper-growth and radical scalability, global hiring freedom, elimination of single points of failure, and much, much more.

Without ever really setting out to, the remote pioneers created a powerful model for how every contemporary business can operate and compete, whether in an office or not, computer-based or not, international or not.

In fact, the Async Mindset is a reimagining of the very meaning of work, with the accent shifted toward the centrality of deep focus—the stuff that creates productivity, clarity, measurability, scalability, and, yes, even human happiness.

As Marc Andreessen, world-famous tech investor, recently wrote in a blog post, remote work may be "a permanent civilization shift . . . a consequence of the internet that's maybe even more important than the internet itself."

Like the birth of agriculture, the printed word, manufacturing, and industry, the rapid adoption of the Async Mindset is not just a trend, it's one of the major reboots in human history, likely to affect everything in its wake.

Once you get the mindset in place, the method quickly follows. One thing's for sure: It's going to affect the way you do business.

> **Remote work processes have freed the organization from space and time. The Async Mindset is the philosophical underpinning required to cultivate and facilitate that freedom, and it's the remote pioneer's greatest invention.**

The Async Mindset may have been birthed by the pioneers, but make no mistake, it's not just for the coders, the techies, or the so-called knowledge workers. It's a giant leap toward greater work sanity for everyone.

Whether you're running a fleet of trucks, a hospital emergency room, or a radish farm—even if you're the sole proprietor of a one-person operation—you have priceless lessons to learn here. The Async Mindset is about building replicable processes that give innovators, employees, and teams real autonomy. The Async Mindset is also about eliminating managerial waste, useless hierarchies, and vanity metrics—the demons that bog down every kind of operation.

Async is the wave of the future, for most organizations. Whether you deploy these lessons in an office is utterly beside the point.

> **Asynchronous Management:** The practice of leading individuals or teams without simultaneous or synchronous communication. All collaboration and information are funneled through online systems. Work focuses on individual autonomy, allowing all team members to maximize their own productivity without being dependent upon others to complete a task or provide updates. Asynchronous management requires process documentation, asynchronous measurement of goals, and the discipline to optimize work efficiency.

BEYOND THE WATER COOLER

It's no accident that experienced, *remote-first* companies—those organizations who choose to work remotely as their primary mode—are some of the fastest growing entities of the last decade, with team members reporting greater-than-average commitment and satisfaction, and profits going through the roof. To cite just one startling example, Coinbase, the first company on Nasdaq to list its location as "nowhere," debuted at $65 billion with an implied market capitalization of about

$141 billion as it entered the S&P 500 at number 89. The wildly successful cryptocurrency exchange platform—started in 2012 by a former Airbnb engineer and, ironically, a former Sachs trader—is a harbinger of things to come.

To underscore what we mean, here are some stats[1] we found about remote-first companies in the aggregate.

- On average, remote-first companies are 22 percent cheaper to operate than their on-premise counterparts.
- 77 percent of remote employees say they're more productive when they work remotely.
- 80 percent of remote employees experience less stress when working remotely.
- Companies that work remotely have a 25 percent lower employee attrition rate.
- 25 percent of remote employees would take a 10 percent pay cut to continue to work remotely.

Can your organization match these numbers? Read this book and, with your help, it will.

> **From governments to housing contractors, everyone is in the process of "going remote," but the ones that have actually flourished in remote mode are those that have adopted the Async Mindset so critical to move, act, and scale.**

In the last year and a half alone, we've seen Fortune 500 companies that vowed to never go remote eat their words and succeed in the process. It seems like only yesterday when billion-dollar unicorn start-ups told us that remote simply would never work for them. Today, with our guidance, they're in the process of permanently shutting down their offices after making the switch.

In spite of indisputable successes in many far-flung arenas, a number of misconceptions about remote work have prevailed and festered, undermining even those companies with the best intentions. Some of these myths are understandable, some ridiculous. You'd be amazed how many people drag them along, from high-level CEOs and founders to whole swaths of middle-management, contract laborers, and beyond.

Here's a quick glimpse at the most recurring hesitations, delusions, and misunderstandings:

- What's work life without serendipitous encounters at the water cooler that lead to creativity and innovation? What's work life without face-to-face meetings?
- How can you have a healthy disagreement remotely, let alone allow for creativity and growth?
- Sure, maybe working async is good for small companies, but not for corporations or fast-growing unicorns, right?
- Isn't the whole remote thing really just about tech jobs and "knowledge workers"? What if you aren't a member of the Silicon Valley elite?
- If you can't actually see your employees, you probably can't manage them well over the long term, right? How can you possibly trust them?
- Collaboration doesn't work async—how can it? They're practically antonyms!
- Employees and employers secretly hate remote work.

- Serious companies require the hierarchy implicit in an office environment.
- Worst of all, isn't working remotely almost like living under house arrest? Doesn't your work life become your home life?

On the surface, these distortions are intimidating. Remote work can appear cold, even alien when you don't know how to harness the unique power of the Async Mindset. To make matters more complicated, some believe remote work stifles productivity and disrupts processes when mishandled—a chilling proposition when profits are at stake. The truth is, some companies do fail at remote work, especially when forced into an instant, all-encompassing transition without guidance. They lose their drive, their mission, and their vision all at once. Moreover, many people—leaders and employees alike—have good reason to dislike the wrong kind of remote work. It can lead employees to feel frustrated, micromanaged, taxed to the max, out of their element, and deeply alone.

Meanwhile, the remote pioneers and their teams are thriving, personally and professionally, and they have been for decades—long before the pandemic. What do they know about remote work that you don't know?

This book is going to spell it out—the nuts and bolts of their secret advantage. It's our great pleasure to share the wealth of information we've nurtured for almost a decade.

Although we're partners in two ventures that have revolutionized remote work across the globe, neither of us set out to be remote workers, let alone remote pioneers.

Liam was a professional-level Canadian ice dancer, one of the top fifty in the world. (Yes, we're talking about the kind where you lift young women in Spandex while doing figure eights.) During the 2001 National Championships in Canada, a bad knee injury took him off the ice, and he subsequently got a job selling water coolers door to door—the most grueling "on-premise" job a person could imagine. Still, the combination of experiences taught Liam about the relationship between process and perseverance. He started planning his entire year in elaborate systems that allowed him to grasp the power of measuring everyday life, right down to how many of his favorite T-shirts would be available on which continent and when he should order them. He subsequently earned a master's in sociology and did a short stint as a university lecturer, which led him to develop an online tutoring business that required a way to track teacher-student hours.

Meanwhile, Rob was a medical doctor from Australia. Pulled by an even higher calling, he left medicine and traveled the world for more than five years, never spending more than three months in any single country. A student of multiple religions, including Osho and Christianity, Rob is an avid explorer of the spiritual side of work and once even spent a year trying to meditate every day for the entire day. The practice changed the way he thought about the workday. At one point, feeling disconnected from what seemed to be the "average" experience, he yearned to give location-based work a try. To that end, he enlisted an Australian software firm with a local office and a local team, just to see what it was like. As owner, he quickly began to question the logic of many location-based work tenets. Working in an office, it turned out, was not so very different from working at home. You sat in front of a computer and did what you had to do. Sometimes you'd even have to email people who were in the next cubicle over. Most of all, Rob hated the commute, and finally just decided to skip it. "If I don't need to be in the office," he wondered, "why should my workers have to be?"

As fate would have it, the two of us first met at a South by Southwest conference in Austin. Liam was speaking on "Remote Work and Process Documentation" and Rob was trying to figure out what to do with his life after running an offshore global team. We hit it off and decided to work together, despite the fact that we were on opposite sides of the globe. By 2011, we'd officially joined forces, creating Time Doctor, a kind of "Fitbit" for work that shows where you put your time.

Time Doctor has grown beyond our wildest expectations, and today we've got more than 130 team members in forty-plus countries, enabling thousands of companies to ease their transition to remote, but this crazy growth didn't happen overnight. In fact, establishing legitimacy in a remote-unfriendly world was an uphill climb. Ten years ago, to start merchant and bank accounts, we had to set up a physical office—it seems like another world today. We still have that office, but nobody's ever been there. As Time Doctor began to grow internationally, the perception that a "real company" required "real employees" in a US or Western office proved to be an ongoing challenge. We battled racism, nationalism, and a general feeling that team-building around the world was somehow faking it.

To make matters worse, a lot of our peers saw remote-first companies like ours as a "lifestyle business," which was a nice way of saying "kids' stuff." (Tell that to Coinbase, WordPress, and Shopify!)

Still, our desire to stay untethered forced us to raise basic questions. From a business perspective, what was the difference between a worker in San Francisco and one in Mumbai, really? What did it matter if somebody got the job done in eight minutes or eight days?

As we grew, we learned to focus on results, and this deceptively simple shift in point of view itself yielded an incredible acceleration. We discovered that async work done right really works. Moreover, as you will see in this book, the Async Mindset provides a methodology that will revolutionize the majority of work in the future.

In time, we made it our mission to educate the world about the Async Mindset and the power of remote scalability. That's why we started the annual Running Remote conference, which educates business leaders on how to successfully run a remote business, with more than 11,000 attendees in 2020 alone. We bring in remote leaders from around the world and figure out how they build billion-dollar unicorns.

Best of all, the conferences have brought us close to a tiny cluster of people who have been operating businesses 100 percent remotely for decades. These remote pioneers are the women and men who have created some of the fastest-growing companies from all over the planet, including breakout unicorns and smash successes like WordPress, Coinbase, Shopify, Doist, GitLab, Hotjar, Vidyard, Conversio, Buffer, Product Hunt, FlexJobs, Fiverr, and many others. They are the primary voices in this book.

None of us went remote as a substitute. We weren't forced into it because of the pandemic or for any other reason. We run our companies utilizing the Async Mindset because we want to. We know with absolute certainty that it's the better, more productive, and more profitable way to go, and we're here to show you how.

IN PIONEER TERRITORY

The remote pioneers featured in this book come in all shapes and sizes, from all countries and walks of life. They've each fashioned a unique lifestyle to match their fierce independence, but the adventure they've been on is not really about lifestyle. It's about how they've all managed to create, build, oversee, and grow successful multimillion-dollar, all-remote companies so far ahead of the curve.

Actually, six of the founders we interviewed for this book are already running billion-dollar companies; let's not shortchange them.

As a group, the remote pioneers are our long-term colleagues and compatriots, and together, we've encountered the challenges and obstacles that many people are facing for the first time as a result of the pandemic. Through painstaking trial and error, we discovered what works, what doesn't work, and how to turn what at first glance might seem like limitations into monstrous advantages.

> **When it comes to remote work, these people have been the guinea pigs, so you don't have to be. They know how to do it right.**

In the extensive interviews we conducted for this book, one recurring fact knocked us out time and again. As different as the remote pioneers are as people, there's an uncanny similarity in the way they think and talk about remote work. Separately, they've all come to some jarringly similar conclusions about how to do it right. That's because, as all-remote entrepreneurs, they've lived the learning curve firsthand. Their time in the trenches taught them not just how to embrace the Async Mindset but *how to avoid doing remote the wrong way.*

As each of these remote pioneers accepted and mastered a handful of fundamental tenets, working asynchronously fueled higher productivity, eliminated time-wasting meetings and treacherous commutes, and stripped away the ugly politics that often undermine the most talented of employees.

Most of the myths about remote work—that it's isolating, that it's only good for companies of a particular size, that it's only right for tech companies—are patently untrue . . . when you do it right. Here are some of their discoveries:

- You cannot succeed by hanging on to traditional office models, expecting them to work in a remote form.
- Successful remote work requires a unique asynchronous/autonomous mindset—the ability to focus on outputs instead of outmoded inputs such as vanity metrics, small talk, and 360 human resources reviews that leave employees fatigued and disheartened.
- The asynchronous/autonomous mindset cultivates freedom and ownership for every participant.
- Remote work thrives on deliberate, purposeful communication. If you're communicating the same way you did when your colleague was sitting in the other room, you're probably wasting time, energy, and efficiency.
- By the same token, those extroverts who have climbed the corporate ladder because of their ability to glad hand will find themselves disempowered in the remote environment.

- Detailed metrics and crystal clear KPIs (key performance indicators) are not only not constraining in remote work, they can free employees to succeed autonomously when implemented the right way. (Conversely, flying blind is one of the worst experiences any employee can have, and it's especially hard on remote workers.)
- Remote work rests on a strong but flexible process—one that not only delineates workflow and keeps communication lines open, but also explicitly conveys company values.
- The remote company is, at heart, an autonomous meritocracy. In general, the async pioneers don't care when you work, or for how long, or how you get it done, as long as you deliver the goods.
- This autonomous meritocracy must permeate the organization at every level, so that process, metrics, and communication converge to empower every player.
- Once you grasp the asynchronous/autonomous mindset, the principles that make remote work shine can also be applied to on-premise and hybrid companies with relative ease.

Some of these you may have already guessed, but some we're sure you haven't—we call those the Counterintuitive Async Bombs:

- Counterintuitive Async Bomb #1: Companies move faster when they collaborate less.
- Counterintuitive Async Bomb #2: Introverts climb to the top in remote-first organizations faster than

on-premise ones, because their thoughtfulness is seen as an asset, not a liability.

- Counterintuitive Async Bomb #3: The experience of autonomy, choice, and participation is actually created by deeper structure.
- And the most important Counterintuitive Async Bomb of them all: Management itself is practically moot in a remote-first organization. The async process, properly deployed, *is* the manager.

Best of all, the Async Mindset executed properly leads to a host of unexpected benefits that the pioneers have all witnessed firsthand.

- Async work tends toward greater inclusivity and richer cultural exchange.
- Women and minorities can reap special benefits from the remote environment, and a whole new generation of leaders is transforming the playing field.
- Async work dismantles useless hierarchies and office politics. No more of "the loudest voice wins the argument."
- There's less gossip when people work remotely. Unlike the traditional office, people are not stuck at a desk for a set number of hours, and they don't suffer the same breed of displaced antsy-ness. Work calls tend to be more focused, and employees are less tempted to waste time squandering their energies with bitterness and triviality.
- Remote work requires a whole new rethink when it comes to hiring and onboarding new employees, and remote-readiness will likely soon be a rated hiring

factor for companies of all sizes. Hiring remotely requires less time to onboard and scale than any on-premise model available.
- In the future, all fast-growing companies will have to hire remotely to be able to scale competitively.
- Leadership has a whole new tenor and practice in remote work. In order to be "agnostic" toward everything but results, the remote leader must learn how to relinquish control as never before.
- A global talent pool means global competition, and instant adaptability is a mandatory survival skill.

Taken as a whole, these ideas are more than a skill set. They are a whole new work language, with some surprising modes, benefits, and challenges. This book is a complete course in that language. We will give you the right formulas to share the Async Mindset and let it grow, so that it can touch every aspect of your venture.

TAKING THE LEAP

It's worth noting that the remote pioneers had to fight their way to most of this knowledge. For many of us, our ventures lacked outside support because we refused to go location-dependent. "Working remote" was confused with "outsourcing cheap labor" by outsiders, and time and time again, we were told, "That's no way to build a business." Fair enough. Our model was not proven . . . yet.

Despite rapid growth, many of us also couldn't get serious capital as we expanded. Moreover, there were legal ramifications to what we were doing, creating what at first appeared to be a hiring nightmare, since every country has its own definition of what constitutes an employee and what constitutes a contractor. Convincing seasoned talent to join our teams often required a real leap of faith.

> **Most of all, we needed to learn not how to equal the office model, but to outshine it, to discover the rhythm of collaboration from afar, and even collaboration without collaboration. Things did not really come together until we made the lack of in-person connection our superpower (in other words, until we discovered the async way).**

This book shares the wealth of that discovery in two key sections.

In part I, we'll illustrate the fundamentals of the Async Mindset by exploring three overarching principles—deliberate overcommunication, democratized workflow, and detailed metrics. We'll show how these principles affect the workplace, the worker, and the company at large. We'll also explain, through nuts-and-bolts techniques and real-life tales from the trailblazers, how these modes differ from old office variants, and we'll demonstrate what new energies they require for a growing company.

In part II, we'll go past the mindset to take a penetrating look at how to develop a thriving async company culture, with a special eye on the true nature of on-the-job autonomy. Along the way, we'll dismantle some of the outmoded old school and Silicon Valley myths about what compels employees to deliver their best, based on findings from the pioneers. We'll also show you why hiring, onboarding, and managing in a remote context is totally different—again with methods and firsthand stories from the founders and leaders who had to do it first. You'll discover that hiring remotely is the way to go, fostering greater success, longer retention, more mutual employer/employee satisfaction, and an easier route to exits when relationships run their course.

When we say the Async Mindset is for everyone, we mean everyone—companies small and large, one-person operations, mom-and-pop shops, and global megacorporations.

We believe that, in the future, every process that can be developed and managed asynchronously will be.

This book will prepare founders, executives, managers, and employees to navigate the new normal. In fact, embracing an async work model is going to be mandatory to stay competitive.

With the findings and stories of the remote pioneers set out in this book, you can master the Async Mindset, to support your charges and enable your company to achieve long-term growth and success. Whether owner, CEO, manager, or employee, you'll find new freedom to thrive outside the old-fashioned restrictions of space and time.

stories from the founders and leaders who had to do it first. You'll discover that doing remote work is the way to go, fostering greater success, lower attrition, more mutual employer-employee satisfaction, and an easier route to exits when relationships run their course.

When we say the Async Mindset is for everyone, we mean everyone—companies small and large, one-person operations, mom-and-pop shops, and global megacorporations.

We believe that, in the future, every process that can be developed and managed asynchronously will be.

This book will prepare founders, executives, managers, and employees to navigate the new normal. In fact, embracing an async work model is going to be mandatory to stay competitive.

With the findings and stories of the remote pioneers set out in this book, you can master the Async Mindset, to support your changes and enable your company to achieve long-term growth and success. Whether owner, CEO, manager, or employee, you'll find new freedom to thrive outside the old-fashioned restrictions of space and time.

PART I

The Spaceless Office: Mastering the Fundamentals

ONE

Lies We Learned in Silicon Valley

The secrets you will learn in this book—work methods discovered and powered by the remote pioneers—represent not only a break from traditional, twentieth-century office models of the *Mad Men* variety, they also mean a break from many of the myths about company culture fundamental to Silicon Valley life in more recent decades.

To grasp just how transformative this change is, think of Silicon Valley not as "the hip newish thing," but as the last in a historic chain of location-based work centers that started with the first-ever villages and grew to include Cairo, Rome, London, New York, Tokyo, and the like.

To illustrate our point, we went straight to the source and interviewed "Josh" at a "major Silicon Valley tech company"—he had to remain anonymous to keep his job.

Josh is the vice president of people (his actual title) for a very successful, consumer-based, internet company whose products you probably use every day. In the middle of the pandemic when we first spoke with him, he reported to us that this company he works for has always been mostly anti-remote. Moreover, he told us that the outspoken CEO has a short list of reasons this company could never go fully remote. For instance, "Designers and product managers need to be in the same space—how else can they produce together?"

Naturally, when the pandemic first hit, panic ensued. The company went remote despite itself and, with jangled nerves, watched for signs of impending disaster.

At first, there was a less than 5 percent drop in productivity, so the Silicon Valley–based outfit searched for rationalizations. "Maybe it's because we're in Q1. We already had a plan in place for Q1." But Q2 was even better, and finally company leaders had to admit that the cost of keeping offices was many times greater than the minor losses they incurred going remote.

For "Josh," however, the change was more than cosmetic—it was a personal life-shaker.

He and his wife had no family in the Bay Area, and it was hard raising their two-year-old without support while paying off a substantial mortgage. As safe childcare became impossible, managing the day-to-day got even harder. His wife had worked at a nonprofit. Now she was out of work and considering a second child. Finally, less than two seasons in, Josh and his wife decided there was just no point in staying. They sold their house and headed back East in the winter of 2020–2021.

Thankfully, the company kept him, and he continued to prosper at his job, but it was touch and go.

What Josh ultimately learned is something we have known all along—that, for the last decade or so, many organizations have operated under a few "soft" but not unharmful myths that grew out of Silicon Valley. Here are just a few:

The Myth: Workers are granted maximum freedom by instilling a culture of previously unheard-of perks like nap pods, snacks, self-focus time, and the like.

The Truth: Perks aren't culture or true freedom. Real autonomy recognizes the individual's sovereign and unique needs and wants—no matter how personal or specific. There are as many different human situations as there are humans.

The Myth: Interconnected Silicon Valley culture boosts creativity by affording workers more time to play and interact with one another outside the realm of actual work duties.

The Truth: Water coolers don't spark creativity, individuals do. Lounge culture is not only less effective than previously imagined, it can prove to be the undoing of an otherwise strong company by setting up a petri dish for uniform thinking and entrenched office politics.

The Myth: Remote work means unhappy employees and deteriorating productivity.

The Truth: Autonomous, asynchronous work delivers both quantifiable employee satisfaction and measurable growth—we see it every day.

It should go without saying that these Silicon Valley myths are no longer trendy news. They've become dangerously entrenched. They're the fodder of "tech bros" sitcoms and ugly headlines, but once you get the myths out of the way, it's possible to understand just what makes the Async Mindset different. Whether you're working from home or from a far-off digital nomad location or doing "collated coworking," asynchronicity fosters a true culture of cooperation, respect, and self-respect.

By cutting out long commutes and fast-food lunches, remote work has the power to bring greater health to everyone involved. It also grants each team member the time and space to put their life focus where they want it, when they want it. But most important, the Async Mindset encourages each person to explore, embrace, and reveal his or her truest self.

That's a perk beyond measure.

SECRETS OF THE REMOTE PIONEERS

In fact, the office as we currently know and understand it has *not* been around forever.

It should come as no surprise that ancient Rome—inventors of roads, concrete, aqueducts, newspapers, sewers, and sanitation—was the first civilization to build proper go-to workspaces in a somewhat organized business district. In fact, the name "office" derives from the Latin *officium*, a term that loosely meant *bureau*, a place for transacting business.[1]

It is amazing that the whole office thing didn't really last. After the collapse of the Roman Empire, the concept went dormant—for centuries. Most work was carried out at home, shop owners usually lived above their workspaces, and the clerks they employed often lodged alongside them.

For most of human history, work-from-home has been business as usual.

The standardized office building didn't formally reappear until the eighteenth century, when Britain produced a few giant structures, including an office building erected for the East India Company, with thousands of employees handling long-distance trading with India and Asia. Author Charles Lamb worked there and gave an account of eighteenth-century office life in all its brutal torpor, decrying everything from long commutes and longer days to drudgery, rescinded bonuses, foul office politics, and even coworker depression and suicide. "You don't know how wearisome it is," he wrote in the early 1800s, "to breathe the air of four pent walls without relief day after day."

The office really sucked back then. And, you know what? It still does.

Twentieth-century planners and organizational psychologists were hip to this malaise, so, they attempted to humanize the office experience, experimenting with a dozen different models—everything from Frank Lloyd Wright's open plan to the "Action Office" of the 1960s and the grim cube farms of the 1980s, mocked as "veal-fattening pens" in Douglas Coupland's classic *Generation X: Tales for an Accelerated Culture.* The lean toward ergonomic compassion was finally taken to its logical conclusion in the Silicon Valley near the century's end, as sweatshop/steno pool formality made way for nap pods, free jars full of jelly beans, yoga classes, and Ping-Pong tables.

For the record, those jelly beans are usually stale, but even more important, how many of those serious ills that East India employee Charles Lamb described back in the dawn of the nineteenth century had *actually* been eliminated? Long commutes, drudge-filled days, stress-inducing office politics, bad eating, sedentary hours, despair, and depression were all still a recurring backdrop to work life for the many.

Paradoxically, the massive upheavals of the information age had as many negative effects as positive ones on office life. In a recent exploration of burnout written by Jill Lepore in the May 24, 2021, issue of the *New Yorker,*[2] it was noted that the

World Health Organization explicitly recognized burnout syndrome as an occupational phenomenon in 2019, many months before the onset of the pandemic. "If burnout is a problem of fairly recent vintage," Lepore writes, "if it began when it was named, in the early 1970s—then it raises a historical question. What started it?"

The article goes on to describe burnout as a kind of PTSD of civilian work life, which "cuts across executive and managerial levels," according to the Harvard Business Review. Long hours, unremitting pressure, high-speed communication, social media, and an economy that never stops have all been whirlpooling to create a burden that falls especially hard on millennials and new entrees.

"Work, for many people," Lepore concludes, "has come to feel like a battlefield."

For some up-and-coming entrepreneurs of the new millennium, the very idea of taking on this standard model of office life was intolerable, no matter the sense of accomplishment or the rewards. As soon as technology began to allow for workarounds, these crafty souls embraced shortcuts and byways without hesitation. They worked new angles, discovered new routes, and, without ever "hanging out," they built empires.

However, before any of them actually succeeded, they each had to learn *first* that nothing short of a whole new mindset would be required to survive and thrive outside the twentieth-century workspace.

THE LEARNING CURVE

A whole new mindset is usually the last thing a company leader transitioning to remote ever thinks about—especially if there's an unknown virus outside that may or may not kill you, your family, and your business. As ambassadors to the remote work world, we've spoken to tens of thousands of remote-first founders and operators of companies in transition, and we've heard every frustration there is. But the one we encounter most often goes something like this: "My company's going remote, doing everything we did back at the firm, and it's just not working. Processes are bogging down, customers aren't getting what they need when they need it, and my best team players are already starting to look elsewhere."

We're assuming that if you're reading this book, you may have had those problems too. Here's the deal: *If you're trying to recreate the office, you've already lost.*

We often meet brick-and-mortar founders and CEOs who want to know if they should use Zoom, Skype, or Google Meet. They ask if everyone's cameras should be on all day, nine to five. Or maybe they can hold "social events" on camera—meet-and-greets or digital happy hours—to break up the monotony. They practice "measurement by presence," equating on-air time with on-the-job engagement, and woe unto the employee who doesn't answer emails on the fly.

Needless to say, none of this works, and there's a reason for it, something the remote pioneers learned on day one: Remote-first work and on-premise office work are not parallels. In some ways, they're polar opposites.

Here's what the remote pioneers discovered the hard way, so you don't have to:

> **To thrive in a contemporary, digital context, you need to throw out almost everything you know about what makes an on-premise office tick.**

Simply put, if you're trying to recreate the office, you'll never make the mental shift needed to build a successful remote team.

As Canadian philosopher Marshall McLuhan once said: "We look at the present through a rear view mirror. We march backward into the future."[3] The old-school managers can't find their bearing if they're fixated on the rear view. Remote-first work is a totally new universe that requires not only the implementation of a new technical language, but the embracing of a fresh mindset driven by unique guiding forces. This mindset touches every aspect of the remote-first business, from the highest conceptual framework to the most humdrum daily operations. To the uninitiated, these implementations can seem as jumbled as hieroglyphs.

Well, we're here to be your Rosetta Stone.

THE THREE FUNDAMENTAL PRINCIPLES OF THE ASYNC MINDSET

This fresh mindset is rooted in three reliable, recurring, and overlapping principles: *deliberate, purposeful communication*; *democratized, open processes*; and *detailed metrics.* Every remote pioneer you are going to meet in this book understands the value of these basics and utilizes them daily as a matter of course.

Without these three elements, you're sailing without a rudder. Yes, you can do it, but it's going to be a very bumpy ride and you just might not get anywhere. Moreover, your competitors may learn how to roll remote before you do, and they will have the strategic advantage of the century.

In the next few chapters we're going to break down these principles in detail, but here are the basics of how they work:

Principle #1: Deliberate Communication

Deliberate, purposeful communication is more than just writing clear emails. It's about coworkers regularly arming one another with maximum data so they can be empowered to deliver maximum results. The greater part of this communication is asynchronous, and we'll delve deeply into why that must be. Hint: It isn't just a matter of convenience or inconvenience. When done right, async is more exact, more rooted to reality, more driven by necessary forethought, and just more helpful and useful all around.

Companies in transition often resist a full embrace of remote, asynchronous communication because it *is* more labor-intensive—in the beginning. However, as a remote-first company scales up, the time invested in building in async mode pays radical dividends.

Taking the time to be absolutely clear when writing down what you want, taking that extra couple sentences to be 100 percent precise, costs you a little time on the front end, but it saves you a fortune in the long run. Short emails require interpretation and often inspire confusion. It's common for email senders in old-school businesses to suggest that the recipient "hop on a call if they need clarification." In async organizations, you send the whole package—the goal is to make follow-up calls unnecessary.

An email is not a preamble to a phone call or a physical meeting. It's a self-contained entity that may contain articulated questions, specific and detailed directions, and well-thought-out conclusions.

Principle #2: Democratized Processes

Democratized processes can only be made concrete through elaborate, "exposed" documentation, bringing the highest level of understanding and independence to every corner of an operation. The chains of events that these process documents describe can feel like a labyrinth to those who came of age in the old-school office, but companies that grow with process documents and grow through them are fortified in a host of critical ways. Best of all, strong process documents eliminate single points of failure, allowing the company to function even when star players are not onboard. In remote-first companies, we love our employees, but *everyone* is replaceable and redundant, and if somebody isn't, you're one step away from possible disaster.

Now, just what do we mean when we say that processes must be democratized? It's much more than "all access."

In the old-school company, only the chosen few could make the rules and laws that helped an organization expedite processes. Almost all large corporations, for instance, have always had clear procedures, but they've had them in the form of top-down bureaucracy.

> **In a remote-first company, processes are created through a bottom-up approach: Everyone is empowered to change the bureaucracy, fostering an organic growth cycle that forces actions to abide by reality, with room for constant course correction and evolution.**

Take Wikipedia. Anybody who peeks into the backend of this 321-language site with 95 million registered users will find a talk section where anyone—and we mean anyone—can make an edit that goes up for a vote. You can even declare that the moon is purple. Of course, you'll quickly be outvoted, but every serious contribution you make will be sincerely considered by the community. The result is a dazzling push toward the democratically elected truth about any topic. Not his, her, or their truth. *The* truth.

Democratic in the original egalitarian sense, remote process-building marks the beginning of a "Bureaucracy 2.0"—it gives what used to be known as the underdog unequivocal permission to participate. In remote work, these process documents are not just for show. Once they've earned company-wide buy-in, they are law and can only be changed by somebody proposing a better version. This allows for an ever-evolving process that lives outside the untested wishes of the business owner, addressing matters on absolutely everything the company needs to scale.

Processes tested by reality get real results.

Principle #3: Detailed Metrics

Finally, *detailed metrics* define quantifiable goals and deliverables to the nth degree, marking a vivid path for achieving them. As with communication and processes, these hard measures can be intimidating to those dragging along an old-school, on-premise sensibility, and that's understandable. After all, who in their right mind wants to be measured to the nth degree, especially if it's some half-knowledgeable middle manager doing the measuring?

Well, in a remote context, metrics are different. They aren't grades and they aren't reductions. These ultrafine metrics clarify and quantify a chain of events so that it can be honed and replicated. They raise employee consciousness by allowing workers to be honest about what their efforts mean to the organization. Once again, with metrics, the truth is at stake, and the very best players are always first to embrace them.

Most on-premise or office-based companies believe they already have quantitative measures, but the majority of the time these are really qualitative metrics, put in place to elevate the importance of the manager. Often these qualitative counts aren't even shared throughout the company. In our organization, anyone can see the quantitative metrics of every single team member, and this form of radical transparency allows everyone to know who is doing what and how well.

It takes courage to play the async way.

Nevertheless, combined, these three principles—communication, process, and metrics—have a seismic effect on the organization, especially with regard to a company's most critical resource: time. The remote-first, asynchronous/autonomous mode grooms an organization to spend its most valued time on high-leverage activities, which deserve that time. This goes for a one-man show, a two-person entity, or a small company, but the compounding effect on a thousand-person organization is near immeasurable and, as you will see, undeniable.

On the surface, these three principles will likely make a certain amount of sense to anyone groomed for the digital age. Still, even in the hands of the seemingly remote-ready, things can go awry when they're mishandled, because it's the mindset in which actions are deployed that makes all the difference. It's a mindset that rests on what first appears to be a paradox: The psychological experience of autonomy, choice, and participation is actually created by deeper structure.

As we meet the remote pioneers and hear their stories, we'll uncover how the very best have used this unique mindset to their advantage. None would return to the old office model if you paid 'em.

LIVING THE ASYNC TRUTH

If the delusions and illusions of Silicon Valley have created a kind of upside-down anti-logic for the working world, the remote pioneers have each, in their own way, had to act like Alice in Wonderland, challenging the nonsensical, pushing past artificial measures and modes.

In the following three portraits, we'll look at three distinct, groundbreaking remote pioneers. As you'll see, their lifestyles are all radically different, but they have one thing in common: their passion for transforming the way we work. They're not just doing it to try something new—they're doing it because our current reality demands it.

Darren Murph, Remote Pioneer: For the Love of Mulch

> "What going remote really exposes is that micromanagement—and management by walking around and checking in on everyone—was never ideal."

Darren Murph, head of remote for acclaimed web-based DevOps life cycle tool GitLab—currently valued at more than $14 billion—has a vision for the remote future and the emotional havoc it can stir up, and it's rooted in the past.

"Imagine," he says, "the first day of work for someone at Ford, on the first day the assembly line was turned on. They were used to building cars with their hands. They didn't know what *adjusted time* meant. Or a *supply chain*! You don't think they had to go through some unlearning?"

Murph's vision is no fantasy. In fact, it's taking hold faster than you can imagine. As of April 2021, Ford itself has also gone permanently remote for all its white-collar staff. That's right. The Ford Motor Company. It's no surprise that Murph knows a thing or two about reeducation. A fast-thinking champion communicator moving way ahead of the curve, he has literally broken the Guinness World Record for "most prolific professional blogger." He'd already composed 17,212 individual contracted blog posts for Engadget.com as far back as July 2010, each with an average word count of 266. That's an average of two blog posts per hour, 24/7, for four straight years.

Frankly, if that were Murph's only accomplishment, we'd be pretty blown away, but it may not be a coincidence that he's also a major figure in the world of remote work. As an early adopter with the gift of gab and some very definite ideas about why remote work is superior, Murph is many things at once: a pro, an expert, a guide, a historian, and an important prognosticator. CNBC calls him "the oracle of remote work." We think a better name for him is "the Wikipedia of remote work."

Despite this almost revolutionary zeal (and his apparent ability to type at lightning speed), thirty-five-year-old Murph is the picture of easygoing. On the day we spoke to him, he was planning to hitch a trailer to his truck after our meeting, so that he could drive down to the local nursery and score a couple bags of mulch. In typical Murph fashion, he tied it all back to the power of remote.

"My wife and I are going to do the flower beds this evening," he explained. "And that's super-liberating. I know that nothing synchronous is going to derail this simple nugget of life."

Back when the world was squarely on-premise, Murph held an MBA in supply chain and logistics, but he wanted to explore how far he could go in life without staying in one place. "I have wanderlust in my DNA," he explains—an inclination we've heard from more than a few pioneers. Murph scored a gig covering the launch of new iPhones while traveling the globe, hitting most continents and all fifty states over a five-year period.

In the process, he evolved into a groundbreaking tech communicator. He quickly discovered that working remote and *staying* remote was, as he describes it, "life's greatest cheat code"—a way to knock off your bucket list before growing old.

Jump to the present where Murph finds himself in the unruly position of being the voice of remote for a post-pandemic world. "I get so many calls—from universities, team leaders, consulting firms—and they all want to know: *How do we build team culture? We're trying to do virtual happy hours and all that, but our team is eroding or falling apart at the seams.*"

What Murph prescribes is not always what corporate leaders want to hear. He tells these titans of industry that the more you empower a remote team to *not* be at work, the stronger your work culture becomes, another essential remote-first paradox. Murph contends that an atmosphere that allows people to get their work done efficiently creates a space for everything else—from family, neighbors, and community to shopping for mulch. Working remote makes people want to connect to *where they are,* and that deeper connection reflects right back to a stronger allegiance to the company.

"When you allow people to make a meaningful impact in their local communities," Murph told us, "they pour way more actual *culture* into their workplace. Instead of twenty people moving to Phoenix and living the same basic lifestyle, now, on a twenty-person Zoom call, I'm getting glimpses of North Dakota and Kenya and New Zealand and Copenhagen all at once. They each bring with them a part of the world that looks nothing like your backyard."

> **The way Murph sees it, this cross-cultural enrichment is not simply good nature or inclusivity. It strengthens the organization by encouraging and even insisting that every player get proactive about his or her own destiny.**

"What going remote really exposes," he says, "is that micromanagement—and management by walking around and checking in on everyone—was never ideal. Going remote puts the onus back on leadership to write down what success looks like for their direct reports, and then equip them with the tools and processes they need to pull it off."

Traditionally, managers have had to hold their subordinates accountable, but in remote teams it goes both ways, which makes some nervous—and rightly so. "Some leaders are going to fight this tooth and nail! Many have never had to be accountable this way."

Murph believes that middle management in particular has an innate resistance to going remote-first, and he sees a great reshuffling on the horizon, separating those who will embrace the new asynchronous/autonomous mindset from those who will cling to the old model and likely flounder.

One thing about going remote never ceases to surprise outsiders: The remote-ready Async Mindset favors introverts. These are the people who are most likely to make their contribution to the organization through hard work and concrete contribution rather than smooth politicking.

"In the past," Murph says, "you've had brilliant people in the world that could never make their way up the corporate ladder, because they never felt comfortable being the most boisterous, the loudest voice in the room. So, the result was that you had leaders that were worthless as leaders, but they got to where they were because they knew exactly what to say, how to be a big voice in a room, how to tie their tie a certain way. And it was useless—vanity metrics."

The Async Mindset undermines vanity metrics by taking the focus off individual charisma, hierarchical pressures, and intimidation tactics. Bad news for some: In remote, you're only as good as your measurable results, corroborated by asynchronous data.

Senior leaders who once deployed conventional command and control tactics are facing a monstrous destabilization of their power at the hands of async, and the loss is more than strategic, it's also psychological. As Murph puts it, "The change is going to terrify some leaders who have essentially shouted their way to the top."

As the oracle of remote work, Murph sheds light on a key element of the psychological shift that the remote mindset requires: the move away from ego and importance-of-self toward egoless contribution and even replaceability for the community good. As he describes it, asynchronicity demands that every single actor makes absolutely sure he or she will not be a single point of failure. It's a counterintuitive concept, especially from an on-premise perspective where success is almost always awarded to the so-called irreplaceable.

In the old office, someone would inevitably catch the role of superman or superwoman of the group and "rise to the top" where insiders hold on tight to their "sacred knowledge." Everybody in the organization would rely on those insiders to some degree, and if the insiders didn't show up, the machine shut down. To that very end, most business books will tell you to "make yourself essential."

"When you're *that person*," Murph explains, "it doesn't matter how great you are, or how great you think you are. From an organizational point of view, you are literally a blocker. Let's just change your title to blocker."

With business continuity and success planning in mind, over-empowering anyone with "sacred knowledge" is a company risk, but that's only part of the problem. The individual employee's sense of duty becomes distorted when he or she thinks, *I better protect my sacred knowledge, so they continue to pay me.* The arteries of exchange are clogged up, preventing maximum growth.

The way to reverse this damming up of brainpower, according to Murph, is to measure management not by what they execute on their own so much as what they unblock for their charges. "I might not launch a single campaign all year myself," he says, "but look at how much leverage I created for my direct reports—and look at how many campaigns *they* launched."

This ability to put the ego on hold, communicate deliberately, and work inside a complex process for the good of the company, along with the willingness to be measured entirely on hard metrics, is no small thing. It requires a brave and conscious attitude, the cornerstone of what we mean when we say "mindset."

For Darren Murph, helping to establish and explain remote culture has opened up uncountable avenues of possibility, not just as a thinker but as a person. On New Year's Eve

2018, he and his wife adopted a newborn, a decision they had been coming to for a long time. "The more you travel," he says, "the more you just see there's a need. And because of remote, we have the flexibility to be an answer to someone's prayer."

As we will see, the rewards of the remote-ready mindset go way beyond profit margins, corporate efficiencies, or having the free time to score some mulch.

James Rick Stinson, Remote Pioneer: Welcome to the Jungle

> "We need to harness our own autonomy and start designing life the way we want to live it. Remote work starts with autonomy, but it can lead to something bigger."

At the heart of the remote endeavor is a real love of freedom, and this is not just lip service. If the remote pioneers share one thing, it's this passion for cultivating one-of-a-kind lives, guided by their own quirks and idiosyncrasies. Honestly, even if remote work didn't exist, we just couldn't picture any of these people commuting to a square box anyway.

Take James Rick Stinson, founder of Outbounders.com, a wildly successful telemarketing company deploying "callers with American and British English" to help increase sales for corporations worldwide. That's a sufficiently straight-sounding proposition, but most clients of Outbounders.com probably don't realize that Stinson is what you might call "extremely remote"—he's a modern-day Robinson Crusoe, settling the land and taking time off for ayahuasca drum circles and yoga retreats. These days, however, the universe is vibrating through him without chemical aid. Stinson operates his business from a teepee in the Costa Rican jungle, on a laptop attached to a fiber line he hired people to drag through the densest part of the rainforest. Stinson is not doing this for show. He's an avid surfer and meditator—when he's not overseeing a company with employees in Vietnam, Indonesia, the Philippines, India, Portugal, Bulgaria, Argentina, Columbia, Panama, El Salvador, Brazil, Mexico, the United States, and Canada.

He recently told us that he has officially changed his name to James Sunheart.

A fair-haired, wild-eyed dude with a scruffy beard, a ponytail, and a mischievous smile, we could imagine young Brad Pitt playing Stinson in the movie. Originally from Utah, he first developed his company in the Philippines and India, blew the biz open worldwide, and now he spends his time on the Costa Rican surf, riding waves and meditating for whole days at a time (while making a fortune). Stinson is the remote worker's remote worker, but not just because of his wild lifestyle. He is anti-management and anti-control in a way that deeply reflects the philosophical underpinnings of the Async Mindset.

We remember hanging out with James in his Costa Rican villa while we were both going nomadic for a few months, traveling through Central America in 2015. He answered the door naked, followed by two big hugs, immediately asking if we wanted to take a dip in the pool as it was, in his words, "incredibly freeing after a long flight" (which for him was true in more ways than one). Within minutes he was showing us around his estate, which he had gotten in preparation for what he thought was a coming revolution in the United States. The villa had solar, its own water supply, fruit trees, and enough canned goods to last a few months. He then proceeded to tell us how he was going to build his very own cryptocurrency.

Inspired by COVID-19, Stinson has since moved even farther into the jungle. He spoke to us by Zoom while walking his dog, Luna, around his lush, green property, forty-five acres of mountain jungle. The dog was going nuts barking at the cows as Stinson gave us the virtual tour. "We've got a bunch of coffee and banana up there—see that? And down there's a lumberyard workshop, and behind that is a river . . . we're living a little off to the side."

This "Zen village," as he describes it, is his new project, and watching it come together is a little bit like playing Minecraft, but in real life. "My vision," he explains, "is to create a small community with a lot of the core infrastructure you might have anywhere—a place to eat, a town center, a little library, a place to educate. They've got a little church and, of course, the best internet money can buy."

All the houses Stinson is building are technically off the grid, but they offer real shelter and come complete with clean water and electricity for those who want to live there, many of whom work with him. He's also planning to set up an advanced hospital and a place for VTOL (vertical take-off and landing) aircraft to take off and land. "I want to create these villages like franchises everywhere," he says, "bubbles that we can connect . . . a complete network all over planet Earth."

If all of this seems unrelated or barely related to what makes a remote-first company thrive, guess again. At the heart of Stinson's vision is a core belief that people should only rely on operations that are replicable and self-sustaining. It's a notion pervasive among the pioneers—their love of process and metrics is what makes the whole remote thing tick. The way Stinson sees it, in the long term, remote work can ultimately act as a makeover for society itself, leveraging labor and technology for the many, expanding what he calls "life assurance."

"I'm a freedom chaser," he says, "and I'm looking for something bigger than financial freedom. I'm trying to create ecosystem freedom."

This broad, daring vision didn't come to him overnight.

At twenty-five, Stinson found himself stuck in Manila behind an office desk, working sixteen-hour graveyard shifts to match US time zones. He looked in the mirror and noticed that he was prematurely balding. He saw his life like a bad loop locked into endless repeat, and in a fit of pique he quit his job and headed for Europe, traveling around on trains with a BlackBerry, booking stays in hostels. He realized very early on that "time freedom" was more valuable than any other kind, and so he began to grow a company that placed a premium on saving time. As their marketing copy for potential employees puts it, Outbounders.com is "a virtual workplace minus the inefficiencies of traditional office-based work. Jobseekers can now say goodbye to lost hours."

As Outbounders.com quickly grew, Stinson began to intuit a great cultural shift on the horizon, long before any pandemic. He imagined a culture, or subculture, where people would ultimately value time, along with health and self-determination, over traditional corporate success measurements like profits and popularity ratings. That's why, although he's made his fortune through tech, Stinson learned to limit his own use of the phone and laptop as much as possible in order to better slow time down. "We have to allow ourselves to be bored again," he says, "so we can be creative."

This deep respect for the power of idle time is another one of remote's great paradoxes, and something we'll explore in-depth in later chapters.

"See," he says, traipsing through the jungle with his leashless dog, "there's a real reset that we all need, and it's not just economic. We need to harness our own autonomy and start designing life the way we want to live it. Remote work starts with autonomy, but it can lead to something bigger, which is the idea of sustainability and sovereignty, both as individuals and as a global network of communities that can operate autonomously and make decisions for themselves. And it's *happening*—" He stops to admire the glorious view and lifts his phone to share it with us, the rolling fields ending in a cascade of banana plants. "That's what's interesting about these decentralized currencies—they're operating autonomously, separate from central banks. It's happening."

Unlike Colonel Kurtz, however, Stinson swears that he himself doesn't want to "lead the village." He is open to an open council and complete feedback to make better decisions, a methodology that stems directly from remote work as we will explore later.

In fact, James has an idea for a celebration for each citizen, a CoroNation, as he puts it, where people can become a sovereign being, their own king or queen.

Digital Nomad: Individuals who travel the world while working remotely—either for themselves or for an organization.

Ken Weary, Remote Pioneer: Global Nomads

"The companies that we would all want to work for are the ones that value the transparency and freedom that remote naturally offers—but big freedom requires big discipline."

If Stinson and his village of kings and queens represent one wild branch of the possible choose-your-own-adventures async work can allow for, Ken Weary and his family are a shining example of another—a case of true digital nomadism in action. He and his wife and two children have lived in thirty-plus countries (!) for the last six years while Ken is the COO (chief operating officer) for the renowned remote-first website analytics company Hotjar. As he puts it, "As far as my employer is concerned, where I am is totally irrelevant."

Often, the Weary family will pick a central spot—say, Marrakesh—and visit as many adjacent places as they can during off-hours. The pandemic initially separated Ken from his wife and kids for four long, frustrating months—he had advanced to Portugal and they were stuck in Seattle. By the time we spoke with him, however, the foursome had been reunited and were living happily in Vale Do Lobo, just outside Faro on the southern coast of Portugal, albeit in lockdown. The Atlantic wind was whipping around him as he chatted with us in front of the bluest sky you've ever seen—nothing virtual about it.

The Wearys are not alone. In a new, original research study, A Brother Abroad reports that there are more than 35 million working digital nomads currently traipsing the globe for an average of 6.1 years, with more than 85 percent on the road for longer than a year.[4] MBO Partners, in its most recent report, shed light on the nomadic profile: While digital nomads do skew young and male, one-third are female and 54 percent are over the age of thirty-eight. Creative professions dominate, but IT and marketing are also strong participants in the movement. One in six earns more than $75,000 annually, although this group is split relatively evenly between full- and part-time workers.[5] They're out there, they're working, and they're making it work.

Ken warns up front that digital nomadism isn't for everyone. A couple he knows recently went to pieces after one short month mixing work and travel. The Wearys know how to keep it manageable, in part, because they've withstood the trials and learned some tricks along the way. Bad Airbnb experiences have taught Ken to bring his own router, because he doesn't want to daisy-chain into whatever is running through each new house, apartment, or hotel. He also carries along a mesh-distributed eero network to make sure he can access any nearby Wi-Fi. His family has also learned to buy individual SIM cards so they can communicate locally without hassle. The kids initially started at an international school in Guatemala, but now they're both learning online at Galileo (https://galileoxp.com), an educational website with a deeply embedded remote philosophy that centers on the power of avant-garde, personalized, self-directed learning.

It's a rich and colorful life they're leading, but every new stop has its challenges. Wherever they travel, Ken's twelve-year-old son, Tag, asks, "Can we flush toilet paper here?" A host of other questions have to be answered, front and center: Can we drink the water? What do you do with the trash? And that old classic, Where's the nearest grocery store? His sixteen-year-old daughter, Ela, also wants to know where and when she can pick up her Pilates and Krav Maga classes. They've been on the road since ages five and nine, respectively.

"We dial it in pretty quick," Ken says. "As soon as we hit the ground, we have different responsibilities."

You can catch a play-by-play account of many of these adventures on their charming blog, Sunglasses Required (https://www.sunglassesrequired.com), which features some useful tips and tidbits for the globe hopper set. Around the time of our interview, they had recently applied for residency in Portugal, so that they'd have no limitations coming and going through Europe, with their sights set on a multi-month road trip through Spain.

But when do the Wearys intend to stop all this re-re-relocating and finally "settle down"?

"Well," Ken says and smiles, "not anytime soon."

He explains that being "location independent" means different things to different people. There are those who do digital nomadism as an Instagram-driven fling, and those who are Nomad Lifers, bouncing from country to country a month or two at a time, in perpetuity. He also sees an interesting split between those locals who have no idea what the heck he does for a living and the embedded "nomad subculture," in other words, the places in each town where digital workers from all over the world congregate. "In Tbilisi, I had to have my meetings on a park bench, because the bed and breakfast didn't have good Wi-Fi," he told us. "The locals walking by thought I was a weirdo."

Maybe so, but there's nothing kooky about the work he does. Hotjar provides the data that help people and companies understand precisely how visitors are using a given webpage, anonymously analyzing their behavior in minutiae: How many people are scrolling down on that first page to read below the fold? Where are they clicking? Where are they not clicking? Through anonymous recorded sessions, Hotjar can follow users' paths, watching them go from page to page to see how they interact with a website as a whole, as well as between websites. By identifying what people actually engage with and what they ignore, Hotjar delivers the hard metrics that make real course correction possible.

One critical mind-state Hotjar tracks is confusion: Why did twenty users ignore the pop-up they were likely looking for, and what inspired them to subsequently take a wrong turn? By isolating those points of ambiguity that are hidden in every design, and by cleaning them up for optimization, Hotjar is a trailblazer in the very values of communication, process, and metrics that make the Async Mindset so hyper-functional.

In part because of this work, Ken is a blackbelt at managing remote teams. He previously ran a US-wide distributed work-force for more than a decade, and the two contrasting jobs have made him keenly aware of the possibilities and limitations when humans are confronted with digital space. "We're making [work life] more collaborative, more enhanced, more data rich, with more shared decision-making. And I would say any brick-and-mortar business should probably be thinking about doing that as well, because the tools and processes that will enable them to do so are in place."

Ken has put his fine mind to the big questions about remote work. "How do you monitor workforce efficiency?" he asks. "Well, not by *looking* at people! And if you still do that in your current office, you're probably not in good shape. It's not only worthless; it's harmful."

He observes that the most successful companies that exist—"the companies that we would all want to work for"—are the ones that value the transparency and freedom that remote naturally offers . . . but big freedom requires big discipline. Weary's busiest days are filled with Scrum meetings where departments come head to head like rugby players to figure out how to move the ball forward. One key aspect of these meetings that is germane to the remote mentality: You're *only* allowed to present problems or ask for help. The goal is maximum data, minimum wasted time.

"You're not there to give a status," Ken says. "No *'Oh, well, last week I did this and yesterday I did that and there's this really cool thing, let me show you.'* Nope. The Scrum Master is there to keep the ball rolling."

The key to these meetings is the advanced deliberate communication all participants provide and receive. If substantial materials aren't delivered in advance, that topic is scratched from the meeting. "Why even discuss it?"

On the day we spoke to him, Ken had just received materials from a colleague about hiring on a continent they had never recruited from before. This coworker had teed up a brief pre-pitch to Weary and a handful of other execs that basically stated, *I'd like to start hiring in this place, and here's my plan.* However, it was quickly determined that the decision could affect the working dynamics of the whole company, and Weary's counterparts in sales, marketing, and product needed to be apprised. Before a senior executive meeting could be called, the colleague had to send out advanced reading via Discourse, including a threaded conversation with links to hard numbers and facts that built her business case. The debate itself could take place asynchronously, with all questions, ideas, affirmations, and objections presented and volleyed before anybody wasted a single minute on Zoom. You could even watch the videos presented at three times the speed (complete with chipmunk voices), if you wanted.

Maximum data, minimum wasted time.

Ken notes that these asynchronous processes are set up primarily because they underscore the company value of *Work with respect.*

> **Sync or async, the push is always toward clarity, comprehension, and resolution, and certain modes naturally complement this push.**

For instance, what people say on chat is usually top-of-mind and seldom as well thought out as it could be. When chat becomes fodder, it ceases to be harmless—even seemingly innocent fodder can become toxic to productivity. When Slack and email chains start to build up and turn into that fodder, Weary or his peers may jump in and say: "Hey, time out. Move this to a better medium."

Ken is quick to point out that this level of "shared communication consciousness" isn't just managerial—he expects it from every single member of his team. "If you're wasting a ton of people's time, going off on diatribes, I'm sorry, somebody in your group needs to call you out. It's a shared accountability."

Hearing Ken speak so eloquently about it all, it's jarring to suddenly remember that he's just a guy without a desk, talking into his phone on a sunny, seaside balcony in Portugal. And yet, this juxtaposition is precisely what he's all about—the beauty of global freedom meeting the power of global teamwork.

He's also quick to point out that all of this describes Hotjar's desired norms and behaviors. "No one in the company is perfect when it comes to them. Everyone does their best, and that's what makes it work. It's easy to fall back into natural habits from traditional face-to-face work settings but if everyone is trying, everyone is learning, and it creates a strong reinforcing function."

If Darren Murph is the Wiki of remote, and James Rick Stinson aka James Sunheart is a kind of philosopher of remote, Ken Weary is something else entirely—a smart man going remote because it just makes good, practical business sense. He knows, for instance, that one of the giant strengths of async is the way it positively affects recruitment, interviewing, hiring, and training, a topic we explore in depth in chapter 6: "On-ramping the Remote Worker." At Hotjar, newcomers are initially invited into the Slack community to interact with current employees in real time, thus giving potential members a taste of what it's like to be "within" Hotjar, so they can experience their unique collaboration style. The team simultaneously gets all kinds of "tells," "affirmations," and occasionally "red flags" from the participating candidate—*How much do they engage? How useful are those engagements? How much guidance do they require? How proactive are they about seeking solutions?*

Weary will often onboard the prospects with small paid projects, to test the waters. "I've got to work with you before I can *work* with you," he says. "I'll pay you—but let's see how we really go together, a try-before-you-buy contract."

We reckon that this testing of the waters would be harder to pull off in an on-premise office. The very act of entering a formal workspace adds gravity to the employer-employee relationship, especially when thousands of dollars' worth of HR recruitment and managerial training have been invested. At Hotjar, the sense of autonomy cuts both ways. Once or twice a year, a freelancer will say: "You know what? This just isn't right for me. I'm going to bow out."

Nothing could make Weary happier. "You say, 'Awesome, here's the money for the deliverable you didn't finish, we wish you well.' Because they have saved us so much time. What if we had moved forward and they faked it? That would have been very costly."

Weary is optimistic about the future of async. He believes that the most forward-thinking companies are already looking to the remote pioneers for solutions, and he points to the new tech developed in response to the pandemic.

"It's not an overnight shift, right? You need to recognize that some managers have developed a bias over the course of their career, and it needs to be corrected. They may not even know that the tools and the processes exist. How do you hire in a remote environment when you've never done it before? Their growing pains are real."

In our next three chapters, we'll hunker down and take on the three recurring fundamental principles of remote work—deliberate, purposeful communication, democratized workflow processes, and detailed metrics. We'll explore the who, what, where, when, and why of each, so that you can bring your organization into the evolution/revolution with complete confidence.

Distributed Work: Any operation whereby the entire team is geographically spread across multiple countries and time zones, without a central office.

ASYNC'S TRUE NORTH

In many of our key endeavors, the remote pioneers are forever striving for total async, the utopia every remote company aims for but never quite achieves. It turns out we're not alone.

Matt Mullenweg, a remote pioneer if there ever was one, is the founder of Automattic, the company whose brands include juggernauts like WordPress, Akismet, Gravatar, and Tumblr. Mullenweg built an international empire without ever setting up shop in the traditional sense, and the important work he's done in the digital sphere has been underscored by his brilliant analytic work. Once referred to in *POWER* magazine as "the Blog Prince," Mullenweg has managed to build a completely remote company that powers more than 30 percent of the internet. If you've looked at a blog on the internet, it was probably on something Mullenweg built.

In the early days of remote work, Automattic actually had an office in San Francisco, perhaps because of the pressures back then to "seem legit" in the eyes of investors and the tech community. However, years later, it completely shut down the office, simply because, as Matt said, "Nobody was showing up!"

A key proselytizer and advance man for the cause, Mullenweg describes going remote as a "moral imperative" whereby "any company that can enable their people to be fully effective in a distributed fashion, can and should." In other words, he's a man after our own hearts.

In his captivating blog, *Unlucky in Cards*, he defines "Distributed Work's Five Levels of Autonomy," tracing a magnificent thumbnail of the journey that can be made from the old-school office to the Async Mindset.

At Level Zero, you are busy doing a job that cannot be accomplished unless you are physically there. Mullenweg cites the "construction worker, barista, massage therapist, firefighter" as examples, but he's quick to point out that many companies have radically overestimated how many of their workers actually need to operate at Level Zero. We concur: The nurse needs to be on-call. The person who administers scheduling for all the nurses does not.

Inching up to Mullenweg's Level One, the employer or manager has made no deliberate effort to make work remote-friendly. "Work happens on company equipment," he says, "in company space, on company time." The problem as Mullenweg sees it is that these companies, tethered as they are to time and space, have great trouble acting in an emergency. These were the people least prepared for the pandemic.

Level Two is the dark cul-de-sac that most "normal" companies have found themselves in while in the midst of the pandemic: The work itself is still completely synchronous, despite going remote, and everybody's days are filled with interruptions. Even worse, management is fueled by anxieties about productivity, even to the point of extreme micromanagement and over-monitoring. As Mullenweg puts it, "Pro tip: Don't do that! And also: Don't stop at Level Two!"

At Level Three, we enter the zone of true remote-first, distributed companies. Sure enough, this is where "robust asynchronous processes" kick into gear, with an accent on great, written communication and open, shared documentation. If your company hasn't made it this far, you aren't remote-first yet, and you likely aren't built to scale.

Level Four is where the organization truly goes asynchronous. Mullenweg accurately points out that how people work begins to become irrelevant as results take center stage. Decision making becomes more democratic, the talent pool goes global, employee retention skyrockets, and most important, "trust emerges as the glue that holds the entire operation together." Instead of the paranoia and micromanagement that hovers over Level Two, with managers surveilling their charges like gulag jail keepers, the truly distributed entity entering Level Four must develop trust because it's the only chance at survival.

Most theorists would have stopped there, but Mullenweg is a visionary. That's why he identifies a fifth level, a nirvana of distributed work, where your organization can outperform any in-person organization without ever spending one minute in colocation. Critically, every single person sharing this nirvana plateau has time for personal wellness and mental health, creativity and fun. **It isn't just an organizational success, it's a triumph for every player as individuals.**

CHAPTER 1 TAKEAWAYS

1. Major office problems—for example, long hours, long commutes, bad eating and exercise habits, office politics, and drudgery—have never gone away.
2. Attempts in Silicon Valley to sweeten the office experience were superficial—the fundamental ills remained.
3. The cost is a very real burnout that unfortunately includes despair, depression, and even suicide. This burnout has been rising steadily since the 1970s.
4. Everything you know about what makes an office tick has to be abandoned to fully grasp the remote-ready Async Mindset, which requires a leap of faith.
5. These principles are found in deliberate purposeful communication, democratized open processes, and detailed metrics.
6. Deliberate, purposeful communication is mostly asynchronous. It is more exact, more rooted to reality, and driven by forethought. This style of communication is more labor intensive at first, but it sets a company up for major gains as it scales.

7. Democratized open processes are created through a bottom-up approach, where every company member helps shape bureaucracy and procedure.
8. Detailed metrics are not mere grades. They mark a vivid path for achievement and encourage complete accountability.
9. By eliminating "vanity metrics," the remote-ready mindset favors introverts and hard workers over the loudest voice in the room.
10. At its best, a remote-first team encourages egoless contribution and replaceability for the company good.

TWO

Deliberate Async Communication—Introverts Welcome

There's something almost comical about two introverts giving advice about communication. In fact, we're not even sure that we could have become entrepreneurs if we hadn't been born in this era. Neither of us are the types that "own a room" or "work the crowd"—nothing of the sort. Without remote work, Rob would have likely continued as a doctor, and Liam probably would have ended up becoming a lawyer like so many of his friends from graduate school.

Remote work made us. When we think about the lives we might have had without it, we couldn't be more grateful.

Before the advent of remote, businessmen were required to be shrewd in real time in a way that neither of us are really capable of. That's one of the reasons we're so passionate about async communication—we know it's the secret sauce of our business growth. With one of us sitting in Montreal and the other sitting in Sydney, we've been able to build a company—a real, successful, fast-growing company. It's honestly something we never could have imagined had we not tried it, and we want to show you how.

As we've noted, the Async Mindset is really shorthand for a way to understand work that's based on three overlapping fields of concern: deliberate communication, open processes, and detailed metrics.

It should be no surprise that communication is the thorniest of the three elements—the root of the others and the hardest to change.

As even first-graders now understand, all work communication can be divided into synchronous and asynchronous activity. However, even many sophisticated grown-ups can barely grasp the powerful but subtle differences between these two modes. Those steeped in the traditions of face-to-face, workplace communication are especially prone to get it wrong.

Our own formula for when to choose which mode is complex, but it definitely isn't random. Liam likes to call it his "hierarchy of communication." Basically, in-person is better than video, video is better than audio, audio is better than instant messaging, and IM is better than email. As you move up the chain of company-wide urgency, you become more synchronous. As you move down that chain, you become more asynchronous, with discretion.

Moreover, when we choose to go asynchronous, we go *as asynchronous as humanly possible for as long as possible.* For example, we'll exchange ten Slack messages to make a decision. If, by Slack message number ten, we still haven't reached a conclusion, one of us clicks the Zoom video call button inside the app and triggers a "face to face."

The goal is this: We want the maximum informational granularity without sacrificing productivity—our very business rests on it. Yes, we love talking to people, but the fact is we know that chitchat comes with collateral damage: First, it reduces our capacity to get the deep work done that moves business forward. Second, it invites vagueness, the death rattle for every organization, remote or otherwise.

> **In short, for work purposes, we avoid synchronous communication whenever we can, and not because we don't like to see one another.**

COLLABORATION IS WRONG

Just what do we mean when we say *deliberate* communication? It's a whole lot more than just choosing to go sync or async. For us, being deliberate means infusing every form of communication with intentionality and purpose—and that requires deep focus.

We're not robots. We understand that most people instinctively prefer synchronous communication or at least think it's better. After all, humans are, at their core, synchronous beings. We move through space *in time*, facing all the inevitable distractions that real life delivers by the second.

Paradoxically, though, it's this very unorthodox state of being that makes asynchronous activity so special and so useful from an organizational standpoint. As author Cal Newport brilliantly argues in *Deep Work: Rules for Focused Success in a Distracted World*, the really meaningful work can only be done by working deeply—in a state of high concentration, without distractions, with all your energies hunkered down on a single task. For people to achieve the extended flow state of deep work, they'll need an environment that subtracts as much "normal life" as humanly possible, while keeping present all the tools necessary to accomplish their task.

Deep work doesn't just happen. It's like going to the gym—it requires onboarding, practice, and rigorous maintenance. Distraction is the antagonistic force that steals more than the actual moments when it invades your time and space; distraction also manages to pollute the surrounding regions of thought and stink up your general energy state. The phone rings, and you answer. Okay, the call was quick and seemingly painless, but two minutes later—*What was I writing again? Let me reread the last few paragraphs, maybe those were off-track. In fact, I better take two steps back to reorient.* Then, just as you're about to get back to where you almost were, there's a knock on the door, and somebody else needs "just a minute of your time."

Even worse, being alone no longer means that you will necessarily get some peace. As everyone now understands beyond a shadow of a doubt, your main work tool, the internet itself, is a Trojan horse of distraction, hiding a whole economy out there in the wings just waiting to pounce on your time, grab you by the eyeballs, and never let you go. Pop-ups, flashing ads, push notifications—they're as bad as the person in the next office over who keeps coming by to chat. String together enough of those stolen minutes for enough employees in a large organization and you have drained away an engine of potential.

The great pity of it is that most synchronous communication between workers—in other words, the vast majority of interruptions—can and should be consumed asynchronously.

Metrics, presentations, updates, and even brief messages are all much better on your time, when you're ready.

> **Synchronous, on-premise work life is a distraction machine, a brutal chain of false starts that destroys the flow for every individual, all day long.**

Above and beyond issues of distraction, asynchronous communication is more powerful and more creative than the average CEO realizes. It's not just about volume control. Async requires that every participant be as accurate as possible with objectives and results, mastering special techniques to maintain workflow when all parts of a process are not available.

By contrast, a number of remote pioneers with whom we spoke agree that synchronous communication is surprisingly overrated. As Amir Salihefendić from Doist has stated, "Synchronous interruptions are poison for work; they leach off your attention and energy and, at the end of the day, you've spent eight hours doing things without having very much work at all."[1] It may be better—sometimes—for blue sky creativity and group problem-solving, but when productivity is at stake, synchronous communication is rarely preferable. Moreover, it often comes with a heavy price—power-mongering, micromanagement, office politics, and snuffing out valuable input.

We'd love to pretty it up so that we can come out looking like good guys, but here's the cold, hard truth: Communicating synchronously is mostly a big waste of time.

You might want to throw this book out the window right now, but hang tight and give us a chance to explain—we would not say such a thing if it weren't true.

One more time, just so you know we aren't joking:

In the majority of cases, communicating synchronously is *mostly a* waste of time.

So, why, you ask, do on-premise organizations cling to synchronous communication? It's a fair question. You may even be one of those clingers. Here's more cold, hard truth: Most major companies are tethered to outmoded context. They live under the brutal sunk cost of offices and multi-hour commutes. They already signed the lease long before the meeting began, and therefore, they have to justify the expensive corner they've painted themselves into.

By contrast, remote work travels light. The final principle in remote communication is this: Whether synchronous or asynchronous, remote work prizes results over personality. It no longer matters how you work, or where you work; only that you deliver the goods.

On-premise, Flexible, and Remote Work: As obvious as it may sound, these terms are often treated amorphously, but their actual definitions are precise. *On-premise work* describes those activities that must be completed in a specific geographic location such as a factory floor or a chemical laboratory. *Flexible work* can be done at a specific location, but it can also be accomplished in full anywhere else. *Remote work* is utterly untethered—you can do it anywhere you can set up your necessary tools.

Adii Pienaar, the Rockstar of E-commerce

> "The only time I would ever pick up a phone and call someone or even send a WhatsApp message on a personal device would be, literally, 'house on fire.'"

Among its many benefits, async has the uncanny ability to embolden introverts and others who have developed their communication skills in unconventional ways. Where competence, and competence alone, is the key measure, a truly shy person is just as likely to be the next hotshot founder of a unicorn as any extroverted type A person.

To illustrate, we can think of no better example than our longtime friend and colleague Adii Pienaar of Cape Town, South Africa. Adii is tech royalty from the earliest days of remote, with three major wins already under his belt. Only twenty-nine years old, he just "retired" from the last company he founded, developed, and then sold for an amount reported to be in excess of R100 million (approximately $6.56 million). He was pleased with the sale, of course, but then again, a few years earlier he'd already launched WooThemes and sold it to Automattic for a reported $30 million. He's a powerhouse and a force of nature.

We first met Adii at a tech conference more than five years ago. He's almost six feet tall, with a heavy South African accent, and he jokes so much we never really know when to take him seriously. He has a penchant for profanity that can be disarming. It's weird to have a nearly six-foot-tall guy yell across a group of five hundred people at a conference, "Hey, you @#$&! Let's go get a drink!" We actually thought he didn't like us at first, until we learned that Adii has a communication style all his own—fun, sometimes very direct, and never taking himself too, too seriously.

What we ultimately came to understand about Adii is what is perhaps most interesting: Although he's sometimes referred to as "the rockstar of e-commerce," Adii is one of the most soft-spoken entrepreneurs we have ever met, in some ways a genuinely shy or diffident person who tells us he mostly enjoys reading, wine, and beautiful objects, and openly admits to being "totally conflict avoidant."

Where else but in the remote world would an Adii Pienaar shine the way he has?

But just how does this preternaturally shy person lead multiple companies to multimillion-dollar exits?

"You write a hell of a lot!" Adii says. "What I love doing with my team is to always share, in writing, not just the consideration itself, not just the content, but how I think it will play out, and why I believe what I believe. I actually share my thought processes, and link those thought processes back to our values, drawing on other artifacts to build up a case. It's deliberate."

Adii says that while it's important to not always take the "biggest hammer to the smallest nail," the remote leader can never be afraid of being verbose. "I rather like to overcommunicate," he says, "to get the buy-in on those bigger things."

No surprise, then, that Adii thinks of asynchronous communication as his default mode, the mode with which to approach all "me problems."

"I default to asynchronous," he explains in his jovial South African accent. "Like, that should be the start. The only time I would ever pick up a phone and call someone or even send a WhatsApp message on a personal device would be, literally, 'house on fire,' and the only way to put this fire out is if I have this person's attention."

When Adii says "house on fire," he is referring to problems that threaten to go company-wide. If there's a glitch in code that's about to spread to all major departments, or if the main server is down and all the technicians on hand can't restart it, Adii *might* ping you.

"But for everything else?" He shakes his head. "You see, I only pick up the phone for a *we* problem. If there's three or more people affected, if the issue becomes exponential, I go synchronous."

This me/we dichotomy is just one more handy marker for discerning whether to choose sync or async. The key in a remote environment, according to Adii, is being able to distinguish your own agenda and priorities from the actual priorities of the business, the strategic goals that touch everyone around you.

Never picking up the phone to handle anything personal is a big boundary to draw for anyone running a team—even bigger when you consider that Adii runs multiple teams at once, in other words, the whole organization.

For Adii, the me/we mirrors sync/async in uncanny ways. Synchronous communication, he says, creates a kind of self-sustaining entropy that leads to even more, and even less utilitarian synchronous communication. Async, on the other hand, is its own cleansing mechanism. The very act of reaching out asynchronously forces the actor's hand toward a more single-minded, yet more organizationally sound use of time. "When I need to be more purposeful in my communication," he says, "I need to take my personal agenda out of my ask and see what else might be happening."

Async has an especially profound effect on debate and even intercompany conflict. "With async," Adii says, "you're much more likely to debate thoughtfully. When you're not forced to think on your feet and react impulsively to someone saying something, what actually happens is you go out and you find those data points to support what you're going to say. You're not expected to react immediately, so the discussion itself is more robust, with more information allowed in there."

He admits that the downside means it can take longer to get to a big decision when you work asynchronously, but it's also more likely to be the right decision, with more information, more context, and more genuine buy-in.

"You know," Adii says, "it's not my responsibility, as a leader, to always make great decisions. It is, however, my responsibility to facilitate great decision-making. If I start the conversation, I need to make sure that the right people are in that conversation."

As Adii describes it, the async leader is a kind of referee, watching for the progressive narrative in a debate or conversation, making sure the game is moving forward. And when progression stops? It's on the leader to intervene. "If there's a kind of triggering event that brings things to a halt, it's like, 'Okay, guys, async is not going to work out here, the written word is just not going to do it, we need to schedule a call.'"

Even then, Adii prescribes a "very concrete agenda" for such a call, with a written summary of what has already been agreed upon, to ensure that all parties will not be tempted to rehash. When it's time to attack the problem, you do so with finality—one and done. "When you go synchronous, you solve it, and you don't go back."

At Adii's last company, he stopped doing one-on-ones with the teams and switched to everyone doing a fifteen- to twenty-minute self-evaluation in front of the whole group, in order to share their agenda.

"What we've learned is that the other person's consideration is part of your agenda. You don't schedule an hour-long meeting where the first half-hour is like, literally, just kind of shooting the sh**, trying to figure out what we're actually here to discuss, right. That's putting the work on the other guy. Instead, you come out and say, 'Here's the thing that I actually need to communicate.' Like, make this a great fifteen minutes, and do the rest on your own time."

The Apple of Our Eye

In June 2021, Apple CEO Tim Cook sent a note to all employees saying they would need to return to the office three days a week starting in the fall.

A mere two days later, a counter-letter from Apple staff leaked to the press.

It stated the following: "We would like to take the opportunity to communicate a growing concern among our colleagues. . . . That Apple's remote/location-flexible work policy, and the communication around it, have already forced some of our colleagues to quit. Without the inclusivity that flexibility brings, many of us feel we have to choose between either a combination of our families, our well-being, and being empowered to do our best work, or being a part of Apple."

What was striking about the letter wasn't just the courage the employees showed when they decided to step up to their leader. It was also the multidimensional granularity and clarity with which they presented their case—a direct consequence of handling the situation both asynchronously and deliberately. They quite literally let cooler heads prevail.

"Over the last year," the letter goes on to state, "we often felt not just unheard, but at times actively ignored. Messages like, 'we know many of you are eager to reconnect in person with your colleagues back in the office,' with no messaging acknowledging that there are directly contradictory feelings amongst us feels dismissive and invalidating. . . . It feels like there is a disconnect between how the executive team thinks about remote/location-flexible work and the lived experiences of many of Apple's employees."

It's also important to note that about eighty employees were involved in writing and editing this rebuke—another consequence of acting, not only with asynchronous deliberation, but with an open, democratized process—our next fundamental principle. The letter concludes with a series of unflagging statements that read like a passionate political manifesto, and it's a wonder to think that eighty-plus writers were able to share and edit one another into this high level of bold, unwavering fortitude.

- We are formally requesting that Apple considers remote and location-flexible work decisions to be as autonomous for a team to decide as are hiring decisions.
- We are formally requesting a company-wide recurring short survey with a clearly structured and transparent communication/feedback process at the company-wide level, organization-wide level, and team-wide level, covering topics listed below.
- We are formally requesting a question about employee churn due to remote work be added to exit interviews.

- We are formally requesting a transparent, clear plan of action to accommodate disabilities via onsite, offsite, remote, hybrid, or otherwise location-flexible work.
- We are formally requesting insight into the environmental impact of returning to onsite, in-person work, and how permanent remote-and-location-flexibility could offset that impact.

As of the writing of this book, Apple is still remote, holding off on their return to the office, and many other multinationals like Facebook, PwC and Deutsche Bank have all gone remote and async. The dominoes are falling, and if it feels like async is the future, remember that it has its roots in the past. Come to think of it, the Declaration of Independence was a deliberate communication created asynchronously through democratized, open processes. The only difference was they used quills and ink.

ASYNC VERSUS SYNC: WHAT YOU NEED TO KNOW FIRST

A basic breakdown of the differences between async and sync is the best way to communicate why async is so hard to start and so advantageous to your business once you get rolling (see figure 1).

SYNC VS. ASYNC

💬	📖
SYNC leaves behind no history.	ASYNC develops perfect documentation.
SYNC gets muddied by charisma and the loudest person in the room.	ASYNC runs on near-pure meritocracy.
SYNC can get emotional despite best intentions.	ASYNC requires that you always assume positive intent.
SYNC is expensive; in particular, it doesn't scale well.	ASYNC is exponentially more efficient and is *built* to scale.
SYNC is a game of telephone, with all the reinterpretation and misinterpretation that entails. Often the final message is a shell of the original.	ASYNC is instantly transmissible at every level, communicable to anyone and everyone in your org with the flick of the wrist.
SYNC never manages to get the whole story quite right, marred as it is by POV, charisma, non-verbal tics, and all the other stuff that makes a story a little too complex yet ultimately unclear.	ASYNC has the power to achieve maximum informational granularity, also known as the facts and nothing but the facts.
SYNC discussions are usually won by the most extroverted team members (whether they're right or wrong).	ASYNC discussions can only be won by the smartest, savviest, or most articulate people in the game, often those introverts who would never dare speak up in a meeting.

FIGURE 1

CHAPTER 2 TAKEAWAYS

1. Deliberate, purposeful communication is the most essential of the three fundamental principles of remote work.
2. All communication lies on a continuum between fully synchronous and fully asynchronous. Knowing when to choose which mode is the key to growth and success.
3. The goal is to go as asynchronous as humanly possible, for as long as possible.
4. Async communication demands maximum informational granularity, recorded for all time.
5. Chitchat on the fly comes with collateral damage, including vague language and interruptions to deep work.
6. The unorthodox state of acting asynchronously puts each player in a state of high concentration, without distractions, where details can proliferate.
7. Collaboration in real time is overrated, and it especially undermines those team members who do not have the loudest effect.
8. Synchronous communication is muddled by charisma, where asynchronous communication runs on near-pure meritocracy.
9. Async, on the other hand, forces the actor's hand toward a more single-minded, yet more organizationally sound use of time.

10. Deliberate async communication is directly related to open, democratized processes, because it can allow multiple players to participate, edit, rethink, and spot-check one another's work, moving a process toward maximum granular accuracy.

THREE

Democratized Workflow—The Power of Process

Our promise is this basic: the Async Mindset leads to nothing short of a virtual, autonomous meritocracy.

For this meritocracy to function, however, strong *process documentation* is required at every level. The term may sound dry, but it does not mean mere "rules" or musty "guidebooks" of the old-style office variety. Process documents are a living, growing thing, an all-hands-on-deck work-in-progress that opens channels of communication and makes way for healthy remote functionality . . . and serious growth.

Documentation plays an especially important role in onboarding and training new employees in a remote environment, a topic we talk about in-depth in chapter 6. It also plays a critical role in laying out the values of a company. These values are not just the glib jargon of old-school mission statements. They are thematic directives—you base your most important decisions on them.

In fact, one of the greatest remote pioneer discoveries is this: The more dialed in your process, the fewer emails and meetings you actually need. By conceptualizing a company remotely first, the trailblazers learned to streamline the chain of events that makes an organization most productive, eliminating everything that made office life wasteful, dreadful, and drudgeful along the way.

It's important to note that process is itself a form of overcommunication. When we take a business trip, for example, we insist on a process document that makes our responsibilities impossible to misunderstand. Every detail is laid out as if we each had an IQ of 75 or, in Liam's case, 60! These documents must be ridiculously simple to consume, with photos, maps, and details that would seem inane to the average person. For instance, our assistant provides us a photo of the person who is going to pick us up at the airport. Why would you need that? Ever been to Bali's airport? It's five hundred guys with signs yelling at you to get into their van. Us knowing them and them knowing us makes that process infinitely faster. Even worse, our specifications about what constitutes an acceptable meal would drive a normal person crazy—no bananas allowed. But please believe us, it's not that we're a pack of prima donnas—we want this level of detail for all our employees. Laying out all the minutiae helps free each of us to use our processing power to focus on more complex problems and get the work done right.

In a nutshell, process is the ultimate "ounce of prevention that's worth a pound of cure."

THE HISTORY OF PROCESS

We'd love to give full credit for process documentation to the remote pioneers, but the truth is that process documentation has actually been the secret to most large organizations that work. Historically, if an institution was or is long lasting and successful, you can bet it was usually built off processes.

The earliest example we always like to pull from (because we're history nerds) is the Marian Reforms by Gaius Marius of Rome. For the first time in recorded history, large-scale armies went from conscripted men who would fight when the need arose to a standing, professional military force with a process in place. Many academics believe that this seemingly small action was the key that allowed the Roman Empire to last a thousand years.

Let's hope your company lasts longer!

The smart money turned to process right up through the Industrial Revolution when Fordism, or the breaking down of complex manufacturing processes into easily understandable stages, allowed workers to get incredibly good at bolting on a single car door rather than becoming just kinda okay at making a whole car. Much like Gaius, Ford understood that a good process was repeatable and workers could be trained or retrained to jump in on any part of the chain.

A twentieth-century example of the triumph of process is McDonaldization, popularized through George Ritzer's book *The McDonaldization of Society.* If you're a cashier at McDonald's, you don't even need to read in order to run the register, because it's built on pictographs. Every single thing in that restaurant is measured, managed, and documented in a series of these easy-to-understand processes, right down to the small fries and Shamrock Shake.

Unlike McDonald's, processes play a counterintuitive role in a remote-first environment by freeing up the organization for creativity. Once you've thrown a lasso around everything that's repeatable, you're ready to grow.

At the end of the day, process is not just about the lines of digital communication, it's about the way your company translates directives into real-life actions. Whether you're making armies, cars, burgers, or apps, we believe that a great set of process documents makes life better for all involved.

> **Process Documentation:** In remote-first organizations, all knowledge is recorded and categorized, so that any single individual can consume that information and perform any role in the organization, without synchronous explanations of any kind.

MEET YOUR NEW MANAGER

Actually, we could have titled this section "Say Goodbye to Your Old Manager." In a remote-first async-leaning organization, the processes *are* the manager or at least as helpful or more helpful than a manager used to be back at your office. They're doubly important because they not only run the show, they ensure that scaling can take place with ease. When you have your processes in place, there is no manual teaching and absolutely no over-the-shoulder management. Old-school management is mostly a redundancy.

With processes in place, new-school managers focus entirely on helping employees tackle hard problems.

And what if your processes aren't in place? For a remote company, functioning without them is unthinkable. Every aspect of the organization grinds down to a halt, and collaboration becomes even more difficult than it would be for an on-premise team.

Building processes is a unique adventure for every department of every organization, but some basic principles can guide the way.

We recommend you embrace the four D's: Discover, Design, Deploy, and Debug.

First you need to **Discover** the history of the existing processes. In other words, why are things done this way? Have they always been done this way? How did things get this way? Only with a solid approbation of things as they are can you start to improve.

A business friend of ours recently told us a story that perfectly illustrates this lesson. When he was a child, he couldn't understand why his mother would cut the Christmas ham in two before putting it in the oven. When he asked about it, she replied: "That's how my mother did it. Why don't you ask your grandmother?"

Well, the boy asked his grandmother, who said, "That's how *my* mother would always do it," and so the boy went to his great-grandmother. The ninety something woman explained that, in the good old days, the family couldn't afford a larger roasting pan. They had to cut the ham in two to make it fit into the two pans they had—more than fifty years earlier.

Moral of the story: Understand the history of your processes, because there's often no good reason why things are done the way they are.

Once you've got your history in place, you can begin to **Design**, taking the lessons you've learned and applying the Rule of Three:

Do it once yourself.

Do it twice thinking about how you'll process it.

Do it a third time, while building the process.

If you wait till the hundredth time to get down to construction, you'll forget all the little steps you need to succeed. Think of it this way: Would you want a personal trainer who lost three hundred pounds last year or a guy who has never gained a single pound? You can best convey and teach the details of a process right after you've identified them yourself.

Then, you haven't really started until you start to **Deploy**—that is, take the process to your employees and immediately set out to find out what's not working. Don't worry about what *is* working. Don't ask them useless questions like, "Do you like this process?" Push for improvement and let them know their input is invaluable.

Finally, you'll want and need to **Debug**—often. Repeat Design and Deploy stages until you get within a hair's breadth of perfection, knowing darn well that you'll never actually get there because, somewhere down the line, someone is going to chime in and say, "I think I can make this just a little bit better" (see figure 2).

Process documentation includes the laws of the company. You can petition to change those laws, amend them, adjust them, even strike them from the record, but, in real time, you have to abide by those laws for the company to function.

It's important to point out that adhering to processes is necessary. People who break laws are company criminals, and they need to be reprimanded. Yes, there are processes that we

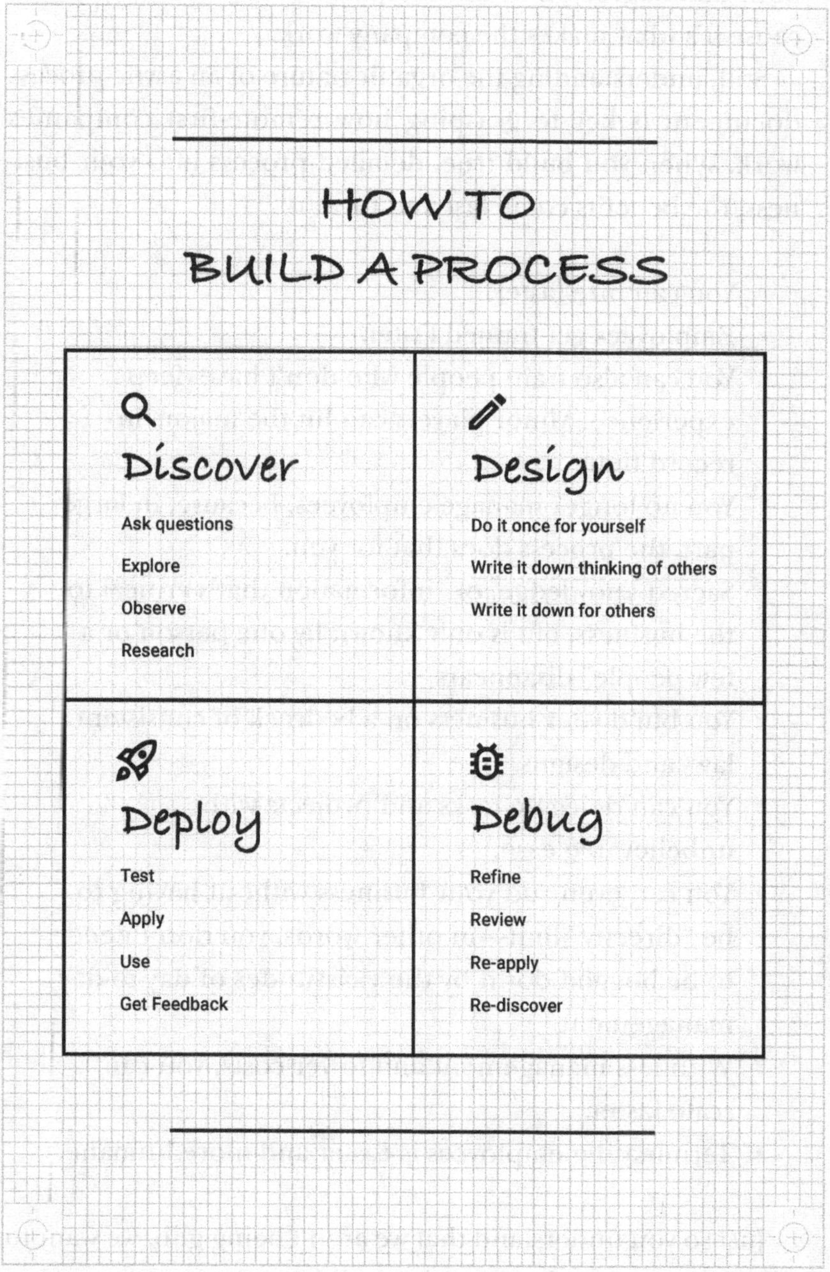
HOW TO
BUILD A PROCESS
Discover
Ask questions
Explore
Observe
Research
Design
Do it once for yourself
Write it down thinking of others
Write it down for others
Deploy
Test
Apply
Use
Get Feedback
Debug
Refine
Review
Re-apply
Re-discover

FIGURE 2

both don't agree on in the company, but we follow them because it's what makes the company work.

Still, understanding the organic nature of an async process document is key to grasping how remote-first companies work. When you build true, detailed process into your business, the benefits come fast and furious:

- You can hire faster.
- Employees get trained faster.
- You can also train people who don't have deep experience. Minor players can hit the majors in record time.
- You no longer manage employees, because, in large part, the process does that for you.
- Sacred knowledge, or "information that's critical to the business, but is only known by one person or a few people" disappears.
- You build your business on a bedrock of consistent laws and designs.
- You can delegate tasks and projects with unbelievable ease.
- You can even run your business without having to be "directly" in it—in other words, you don't need to be bogged down by the vicissitudes of day-to-day management.
- With less management and lower costs, you can scale faster.
- Terminating employees is easier and more humane.

Just so you understand that we aren't being glib, we want to state in no uncertain terms that building processes is a major, full-scale challenge. You must enter consciously, knowing that snags and pitfalls are inevitable. To create the kinds of processes that are sustainable takes about eleven times longer than you usually expect. In general, companies going through a process rebirth initially move much slower, and employees new and old have to adjust to the pace at which a process gets constructed, whether it's comfortable for them or not. In some cases, it can impact company culture.

Creative people are particularly allergic to processes. Even though creative people tend to be the ones who are building the process, there are still times when they want to bend them, break them, tear them to shreds. In fact, at the surface level, nobody loves bureaucracy or being told how to do the job. That's why you, as an organizational visionary, have to help your people understand just how crucial it is.

We know that, without process, our organization will inevitably lead to entropy. That's why everyone—no matter how creative, no matter the size of their contribution—needs to abide by the processes we've set and agreed upon.

As we said, in building processes, you're crazy if you don't expect problems. Explosions will happen. To cite just one example, a few years ago we were trying to make our software more efficient by transferring a large number of files into what's called "cold storage," which happens to be a lot more cost efficient. We spend millions a year on servers, so even becoming a few percentage points more efficient saves us hundreds of thousands of dollars.

What we didn't understand was that it also costs us a few cents for every thousand files we moved. The next morning we woke up to a big fat six-figure bill just for moving files from one place to another—months of revenue for one lousy mistake.

From that day forward, we stole a quote from Napoleon Bonaparte that we still use today: "Orders (or in this case process) shouldn't be easy to understand, they should be impossible to misunderstand."

This seems like a relatively small mindset change, but the results are monumental. Taking those extra two minutes to make a process just a little easier to understand could have saved us from taking a pay cut in order to help pay off our cloud storage bill.

It's worth repeating: A working process isn't just easy to understand—it's also impossible to misunderstand. That's why you need to adjust your lens and craft your processes as if they are being written for highly distracted seven-year-olds.

So, just what does "impossible to misunderstand" really mean? It takes a systems mindset to know when you are not merely "being clear" but inarguably perfect for all, with information that breaks down steps without a hiccup. If a process works nineteen out of twenty times, it doesn't work—yet.

By adopting this stringent testing method, you are really saving your own soul in the long run. When your small company becomes big, you won't be slamming into the ceiling, which just happens to be the number one problem among growing organizations in the digital age. Statistical perfection clears the way for tech, prices, people, and resources, so that you never lose control of your own business.

Like taxes and taking out the trash, nobody wants to have to codify their actions, but once you've taken care of it, don't you feel better?

As an exercise, start by finding the top five time sucks in your day and start figuring out what you can delegate by building a replicable process. We usually suggest taking an everyday activity like answering your emails, and building it into a process using the four D's. Above all, make sure the process is incredibly easy to understand. Test its efficacy by handing it off to the least experienced person on your team. If that person can't make it work, it isn't ready. Remember, if something in your process doesn't play right, it's not your team's fault. Ever. No exceptions.

The way we see it, being good at creating and assembling processes is synonymous with growing a strong business. If you start your business without a mastery of processes, you will probably be unsuccessful, and definitely unable to scale.

And if you know you aren't that good at building processes? Well, then you better turn to the people who've been doing it for a long time.

The Ronzio Brothers, Remote Pioneers: Process Superheroes

"Documentation is the manager . . . that lets you build out of the ether."

We first met Chris and Jonathan Ronzio at a tech event. We hit it off and decided to get to know one another over dinner, where they told us they were putting hundreds of thousands of dollars on their credit cards for ads, since return on advertising for their process documentation app was so high that they could run up a massive bill and pay it off with the profit they made before the credit card came due. We immediately liked them.

This kind of activity would have been incredibly risky and even quite possibly stupid, if it weren't for the Ronzio brothers' unique ability to execute. They were make-it-happen types, our kind of people. We invited them to speak at

Running Remote in Bali, and by the time they showed up, they were already on a trajectory to become a tech unicorn built solely on process.

Jonathan told us that he could spend a full week halfway in Bali because he knew the processes he'd built were so rock solid, they literally ran the Trainual marketing for him. After the Running Remote event, a few of us went to Green Village in Ubud and rented a seven-story bamboo villa in the middle of the jungle. Jonathan spent five days there, cut off entirely from his company, and he never had to lift a finger to keep his operation humming along. We remember seeing him meditating out on the sundeck of this once-in-a-lifetime venue as we were feverishly typing away on our laptops. This guy had it all figured out. We needed to know just how.

"The way we see it," Chris explains, "documentation is the manager. What we do is streamline the complex process of setting up shop so that everyone can work with, edit, and add to the core processes of a company and its projects. It leads to a kind of self-managing system."

Right now, Trainual has hundreds of thousands of processes across its network, including more than sixty malleable process templates on order and several more in the pipeline. Companies of all sizes, including those that are being forced to suddenly go remote, have turned to Trainual to help them codify and streamline. For some, especially those ventures that are not tech-centric, it's been a challenging rebirth, but a necessary one. Getting these systems in place is the building block that lets you "build out of the ether."

The evolution of Trainual is itself a great story about how processes can change and morph over time. At first, Trainual was a product in Chris Ronzio's consulting firm, earning about $2,000 a month in revenue. "It was paying my car payments or my apartment, that sort of thing, and I considered that to be a success."

In late 2017, however, Chris started to get the idea that Trainual could be something they could monetize in a bigger way. He'd been introduced to a copywriter who was going to write sales copy for landing pages, and he knew he needed to drive customers to these landing pages to grow the business. In exchange for copywriting work, the writer wanted 10 percent of any sales that came through. That sounded steep.

So, Chris took a crack at the pages himself, then passed them on to his brother. "Jonathan's the marketing storyteller, the brand kind of person. And he was like, 'Yeah, this is terrible. Let me go and comb through and take a pass at this.'"

To their delight, it worked. Together, they struck a perfect balance, with big brother Chris handling the operations and management like a CEO, and kid brother Jonathan drawn to creative challenges.

"Chris and I have always had a very close relationship," Jonathan says. "It's never been a competition. We always worked together, whether it was car washes and lemonade stands or his video production business in high school."

Jonathan was the kid bro in the basement who learned how to help Chris duplicate VHS tapes on the towers, going on to try his hand at documentary filmmaking and eventually finding a passion for motivational speaking. It was through performance that Jonathan honed his unusually strong storytelling skills—a seldom-explored asset in process-building.

"My brother knew how to tell stories, and I knew how to make money," Chris says. "That was the dynamic. As a kid, he wouldn't leave me alone, so I had to find a way to put him to work—and then he got good at the stuff he was doing."

As Trainual took shape, the brothers encountered all kinds of clients, including companies that were attracted to the *idea* of process-building, without the commitment or hard work that it requires. "The tagline for his consulting company was, 'We help small business owners organize chaos and get things done so they have more time to do what they love.' And that was the capstone that I clung to because ultimately that is the aspiration of any entrepreneur, small business owner, leader. They want to organize the chaos around them so that they can get more done, grow their business while it's not tied to their time."

Trainual has two demos on its website—one for streamlining, one for starting from scratch. It's interesting to note that 91 percent of customers gravitate toward the latter. "Most small companies have everything about their company in the walls and in people's heads," Chris explains. "And the challenge is, how do we start to organize that chaos? How do we add some structure?"

"The ultimate aha," Jonathan explains, "is that the business owner actually knows who does what. That's what we're trying to help them discover and solve."

The Ronzio brothers are quick to point out that they don't deal with resistant companies. If an organization doesn't want to be sold, the Ronzios don't even try, because so many companies are coming to them, 100 percent of which are ready for a change. By merely revealing success stories, most entrepreneurs and founders get the value, but there's an even greater lesson here: Ultimately, process is only available to those who are ready to make a personal commitment.

"It's kind of like doing dishes in the kitchen," Jonathan says. "You just let things pile up and pile up and pile up, right? And there's no urgency to do the dishes until you've run out of forks. Somebody with a drawer full of forks, it doesn't matter to them that their dishes are piling up over the sink. And that's the mindset of people who come to Trainual—they've run out of forks."

Chis laughs at his brother's analogy. "If they only need one fork, they're not going to do the dishes, they're just going to towel off that fork." Then he adds, "Actually the maturity level of the business shows whether they're ready to actually create this playbook for their company. If they have aspirations of growing, doubling, tripling in size, they have no choice."

Sometimes, however, Chris notes that the development of process can expose just a few pieces that need to be moved, to allow for hyper-growth. "When you're on the path to going from five or ten people to having definitive silos of departments with twenty-five people, you're starting to divide and conquer responsibilities within departments. It's not like you have one marketing person anymore, now you have five. What are they all uniquely doing? The division of roles comes first. Then companies need to put attention into their brand, their culture, their company overview and orientation, because that affects everyone. You want everyone moving in the same direction."

By creating definitive departmental roles and responsibilities, an organization can unlock the ability to create alignment, in order to onboard people faster. What every department documents can vary dramatically, but what makes money for the company inevitably comes to the fore. At Chipotle, the question is how do we make tacos and bowls? There can be a ton of other processes, but in the beginning one person is running payroll and the other twenty-four people are perfecting making tacos and bowls. Once the basic procedure is in place and there are multiple people replicating tasks at multiple locations, the unflappable document works like a guiding light.

The Ronzios are quick to point out that not every organization that hires them is ready to embrace getting "processed" at the same rate. "If you're not questioning the existing process," Chris says, "then you're not improving best practices and that will permeate through your culture—your business will stop improving." Chris describes the initial adaption phase as "setting the waterline," the basic level of doing business. Even this initial setup can mean letting go of some unnecessary traditions. "If I write this process down and it is no longer in my head, why does the company need me?" Chris says. "That's the biggest mindset to overcome."

One new customer had a snarl on her face. Every time they asked her what her responsibilities were, she said, "I'm not telling you." Chris is diabetic and wears a wire for his insulin pump. The woman thought he was wired like a snitch in the Witness Protection Program.

Chris says, "I told her, first—it's an insulin pump, but second, I'm here to figure out how you can advance in your own position, make more money, and let go of the redundant things you have to do that tech can take care of."

One thing they're clear on: In order to build processes, participants have to have the shared belief that they want to make the company better, that they want to grow. Snagged by a scarcity mindset, people cling to the very tasks that hold them back.

Some employees are fearful of giving up their sacred knowledge, because they are afraid of being rendered replaceable. In particular, the least talented and least driven employees will be firmly committed to hoarding whatever they think keeps their job in place. It's a regressive cycle that isn't good for the company.

The Async Mindset takes the opposite view: By offboarding your sacred knowledge, you create the freedom to build new avenues of growth that can only add to the organization, while also bolstering further innovation and deeper autonomy. No one process is ever allowed to become the measure of success.

"What if we could take those stupid reports off your plate?" Chris asks. "Don't you want to be freed up to do the higher-level tasks that you're really excited about?"

Ultimately, the Ronzio brothers concede that some things are harder to capture in a process. Creativity, which rests on the unique bedrock of a person's entire life, can't always be translated to a series of documents. However, you can build structure and process *around* creativity, in order to facilitate and foster.

"We have frameworks," Jonathan says. "With those frameworks, it creates space for the ideas when you get together—*what's the concept, how do you storyboard*? can teach somebody how to document a process, around what frame rate to shoot in, what specs to create for ad channels, and how to run ads or publish a blog post, what our voice and style guide should be. But I can't teach people how those ideas will hit their brains or what concepts we should run with."

A Process of Building Process

At this point, you may be thinking, *Well, this all sounds good in theory, but what do these processes actually look like?* Of course, it's impossible to generalize for all companies, but a meta view of the building structure of our own field guide may help newcomers understand how it all works.

You can find the full version at www.runningremotebook.com/guide. Feel free to read from it and steal what works for you.

From the umbrella view, our field guide starts with a FAQ section, how to use the guide, how to amend the guide, and how to expand the guide. After all, if you can't get around, consume the information, and amend that information, you can't really use it.

We also touch on broad categories that make for starting points, including information about the company, information about each department, general policies, and our learning and development plan for all team members inside the company.

Each new layer of process helps the full picture come into focus.

For instance, if you dive into marketing, you'll find a mission statement elucidating the department's core values as well as an organizational chart outlining everyone who works in that department.

Our next section identifies how marketing is measured—a topic we'll explore more deeply in chapter 4—and what targets we've set inside that department. The section includes a live scorecard that can show anyone in the company just how close or far off we are from hitting those targets.

Finally, we hunker down into the specific processes inside marketing, each organized by category.

The entire process document functions like a high-powered microscope, narrowing down to finer and finer activities. Still, no matter how fine, the goal is always complete and total comprehension for anybody with the basic skill set.

Also, each metric feeds into another, so all team members know how their number serves the next one up and the greater whole. When you give everyone access, they clearly understand where they create and provide value to the company.

As we mentioned earlier, processes shouldn't be easy to understand, they should be impossible to misunderstand. Once you invest the time into mastering the expression of those processes, your company will never be the same.

Here's a layperson's illustration of what we mean when we say "impossible to misunderstand." Everything in the following section is handed out to all our blog writers. For the ones who speak Tagalog but write in English, we have a translated version in Tagalog.

How to Write a Blog Post

To review the live version of this process go to www.runningremotebook.com/processes/marketing/howtowriteablog.

Important: Please review how to write a blog post/page if you are unsure about this task, and watch the attached tutorial before beginning this task.

It is crucial that you have properly optimized text for the search engines. Organic traffic is the most important aspect to a successful campaign—the higher that posts show up on search engines, the more traffic those pages will bring in. Please review the following steps, which will explain this task.

Step 1: Log into WordPress at http://yoursite.com/wp-admin and enter the provided login and password.

Step 2: Start a new blog post.

Step 3: Go to the keyword external tool at https://app.ahrefs.com/keywords-explorer and punch in the keyword for which you will be writing the article.

Step 4: Copy the top related keywords into a separate document so that, later, you can use them in the post.

Step 5: Write the blog post integrating those top related keywords into the post, include subcategories with H2 header tags, bold the relevant keywords, link relevant keywords to other appropriate pages, place YouTube videos and pictures that relate to the specific keyword. To confirm quality score, log in to ahrefs.com (online search engine optimization tools) and test the page in question.

Step 6: Place appropriate post tags that relate to your main keyword.

Step 7: Place your blog post in an appropriate category or make a new category if the post does not fit in any of the categories presented.

Step 8: Optimize the post by using an SEO plugin. Write a keyword-rich title tag, write a keyword-rich description tag, write keyword-relevant keyword tags.

Step 9: Publish the post.

To see an example of a running remote blog that has been created strictly within the parameters of our process, look here: https://runningremote.com/non-verbal-communication-for-distributed-teams/.

Letting Go of Sacred Knowledge

As we've pointed out, so-called sacred knowledge is one of the biggest bottlenecks for organizational growth, disrupting flow and stifling innovation. These days, a number of adventurous companies are lowering the drawbridge by allowing innovation to come from outside the normal parameters of the organization itself, letting citizens and all interested parties in on the action. Merit Morikawa of cloud-based idea-management platform Viima[1] recently explored this growing trend, with examples that are far-flung and inspiring. Here are just a few:

- Multinational manufacturing giant Samsung is a proud advocate of open innovation, often aligning with high-energy start-ups for cross-pollination, adding products and processes that create values both ways.
- Medical R&D is costly and slow, but United Genomes Project overrides the usual limitations by using open innovation to create breakthrough medical innovations in Africa through an open source genetic database. Because DNA affects the way different medicines work on different people, the ability to expand the "shareable human database" has revolutionary implications for expanding the boundaries of health.
- Several years ago, Local Motors held a totally open Urban Mobility Challenge, asking all participants to envision the future of transport in Berlin. Today, one of those solutions is a real option—Olli, the self-driving smart bus.
- Everybody knows LEGO—one of the most successful brands in toys. The classic company activates its users through a Create and Share site (https://ideas.lego.com/projects/create) that has developed many legit products including *The Big Bang Theory* playset and the Beatles' Yellow Submarine set. Why should they limit innovation to employees?
- Manufacturing giant Phillips holds a high-tech campus in Eindhoven, which has been described as a "postage-stamp-size Silicon Valley" in Europe, encouraging employees to think openly so that they can harness the resources internal and external to the organization to accelerate innovation or to capture value that would otherwise be lost.

Morikawa wisely points out that the move toward open innovation doesn't merely bring along new ideas, it also fosters motivation among key stakeholders and potential collaborators. That, for us, is the big takeaway: When you open up a process and really let people in, they want to participate.

CHAPTER 3 TAKEAWAYS

1. Process documents are not merely guidebooks or rules. They are a living, growing playbook that opens channels of communication and makes functionality and hyper-growth possible.
2. When it comes to process, you can't spell it out too clearly. It must be impossible to misunderstand.
3. When it's employed properly, good process becomes the manager, eliminating the need for manual teaching and over-the-shoulder monitoring.
4. There are four steps to creating a strong process: Discover, Design, Deploy, and Debug.
5. By Discovering the history of existing processes, you can identify where there are constraints, overlaps, and bottlenecks.
6. Once history is in place, you begin to Design, applying the Rule of Three:

   Do it once yourself.

   Do it twice thinking about how you'll process it.

   Do it a third time while building the process.

   Don't wait for the hundredth try to line up the process.

7. As soon as a process is designed, you should Deploy it—take it to employees and let them find out what's not working.
8. Last but not least, you'll want to Debug your process, over and over, until it nears perfection.
9. Building processes is a major challenge, but the benefits are company-wide, including faster hiring and training, easier delegation, less management, lower costs, gentler terminations, and the chance for real hyper-growth.
10. Expect problems while developing processes. They expose weaknesses in the business that you can't afford to ignore.
11. To establish your own processes, identify the worst time sucks in your day and think about how they can be delegated more swiftly.
12. Not every organization can get "processed" at the same rate. The first hurdle involves letting go of "sacred knowledge," and opening up the playbook for the company's well-being.
13. From the umbrella view, a good process document will let you see the whole company, every activity that company is involved in, and the lucid, easy-to-understand steps that company takes for all its tasks and initiatives. Those with the basic skill set should be able to step in, train themselves, and do the job.

FOUR

Detailed Metrics—Multidimensional Proof

One diehard principle the remote pioneers all agree on: Setting and measuring crystal-clear KPIs (key performance indicators) are at the heart of remote sustainability. In fact, remote work has changed the very definition of metrics, because—counterintuitively—it takes vivid and specific, quantitative directives to set workers free from their managers, so that they can perform at their best.

The remote difference is that metrics do not merely function as "grades" or "scores"—they are the signals for instantaneous understanding of the situation at hand. When your data is in order, you can act accordingly inside a week or even a day versus a month or a year, course correcting where necessary while becoming much more nimble than your competitors.

Metrics are especially important for a company's top brass when they're setting up parameters for self-management. Liam, for instance, didn't know how unproductive his Tuesday afternoons were until he started measuring his own time and flow state with Time Doctor. He quickly realized, by consciously accounting for each minute, every keystroke, that Tuesdays were a hidden problem. On that day it was tradition for him and his friends to go to half-priced matinees or grab lunch, and though he'd usually turn them all down, the messaging back and forth was management itself. That's why his productivity was trashed on Tuesdays. Observing these minor interactions led Liam to simply take the afternoon off, and the amount of work he got done in a week actually went up. But without the measurement of every single activity, he never would have come to the right conclusion.

From there, Liam began to observe how minor work interactions can also eat away at a day. If you're sending and receiving messages that don't revolve around concrete metrics, you're just wasting time and calling it collaboration. We try to get real with our staff and say: "If you want to hang out for the sake of socializing, be direct about it and don't pretend it's work. It's better for team culture if everyone is just honest about how they work and what helps them increase their productivity."

Ultrafine metrics catch minor issues that accrete into major drags on productivity. A few years ago, when we were a smaller company with a smaller support team, we thought people wouldn't message us all that much over the winter holidays, until we discovered—the hard way—just how many support reps were on duty from the twenty-fifth to the twenty-eighth: zero. Despite running a fifty-person company, we were the only active workers, and we spent the entire holiday on the phone apologizing to customers. Liam can remember a long December 26, putting out fires on the phone till 2:00 a.m. You can be sure that mistake didn't happen two years in a row.

The outcome of all these hard measures is that old-school management metrics like yearly reviews and generalized feedback are rendered even more redundant than we already knew they were. In the optimized remote environment, every activity is now its own review, and you know where you stand long before some middle manager tells you so. Every individual contributor inside a company should know exactly what his or her performance is without having to talk to a manager. If someone is unclear about the target or unclear about how quickly to get to that target, both manager and employee have failed.

THE CHARISMA TRAP

When you're asynchronous and remote, metrics are the only thing that can differentiate your performance from the performance of others. Charisma doesn't matter, looks don't matter, office politics don't matter. The only thing that matters is how well you perform on your metric—it's the ultimate meritocracy.

To illustrate by contrast, consider the dangerous case of WeWork's ultra-charismatic founder Adam Neumann. On the verge of going public in 2019, WeWork was tech darling du jour, with a staggering $47 billion valuation. In what was effectively a form of start-up theater, Neumann convinced the largest venture capital fund in the world (SoftBank) to pour billions (that's right, plural—billions) into a company that made less than $1.8 billion a year and was actively burning $1.9 billion a year.

Within a year, all the cards collapsed for Neumann in short order, his planned IPO failed, and the company's promise imploded. The company had claimed that, per square foot, it could double the tenancy of its coworking spaces through AI, a ridiculous notion that nobody in their right mind would have believed, save for the magnetic salesmanship of Neumann, who managed to project himself as an Elon Musk–like visionary with secrets no one else knew. The sorry truth was that Neumann wasn't a visionary, as much as he was an incredibly charismatic cult leader. Thankfully, most realized he was the latter before the company went public.

Just how powerful and distorting was Neumann's charisma? Try to fathom that, even after the entire collapse of his company, he had such a spiritual grip on his investors that they paid him $445 million to leave the company and never come back. That might be the biggest kill fee in human history.

To make matters worse, as his employees lost all their vested interest in the company, Neumann didn't share with anyone even a tiny slice of that almost-half-billion-dollar exit package.

That's your reward for betting on charisma.

Contrast these multibillion-dollar shenanigans with just one of the companies featured in this book, GitLab. Founders Sytse "Sid" Sijbrandij and Dmitriy Zaporozhets are Running Remote alumni, they're very nice men, definitely not Neumann types. That's why we think they'd be the first to tell you that we aren't putting them down when we say they aren't "charisma types" like Neumann. They raised half a billion in funding the hard way—by actively designing their organization to be asynchronous and highly accountable to all investors. For the GitLab boys, the numbers are most important, not the packaging, not the speeches, and not the hype. In October 2021, as we were writing this book, GitLab IPO'd at $11 billion.

That's not $11 billion worth of charisma, it's $11 billion worth of metrics.

THE GOOD, THE BAD, AND THE METRICS

We can just hear you thinking, *But our company already kinda sorta has metrics, don't we?*

To which we answer: "No. Not like we do." In remote-first Async Mindset companies, metrics are a whole different animal.

Traditional companies usually don't even have what we call metrics, they have tertiary data, or conversations about metrics.

Real metrics, when set properly, require no explanation. You can't talk your way out of bad numbers when you're facing remote-first metrics, and since we're asynchronous anyway, there really isn't anybody to discuss them with.

All joking aside, though, you must absolutely free yourself from explaining your metrics. If you have to extrapolate from them, then they are either not simple enough to understand or, even worse, they're likely vanity metrics—useless puffery that you'd be wise to get rid of anyways.

The way we work is different.

> **Every single person in the organization must have at least one metric that they report on weekly.**

Not biweekly or monthly or seasonally. It's got to be weekly.

Every single one of those reported metrics must have an intended target with a significant chance of failure.

For example, our content marketing team has a critical metric called Cumulative Domain Authority—how many backlinks you get for a piece of content you write. A backlink is another website linking to your particular blog post, web page, or YouTube video. These backlinks are the lifeblood of our marketing engine and we measure them very closely, but it took us years to figure out how to measure these backlinks because all backlinks are not created equal.

As you may know, each web page has a score defining its importance on the internet. For example, runningremote .com, at the time of this writing, has a score (or domain authority) of 62 out of 100. A website like CNN, on the other hand, has a domain authority of 92 out of 100. Domain authority agglomerates how many other valuable websites link to your website. It's a kind of popularity vote. This process initially evolved in the academic world, where how often an article is referenced becomes the measure of its impact.

All things being equal, you want a backlink from CNN more than you want a backlink from Running Remote. Needless to say, getting a link from CNN is much more difficult. If you define getting backlinks en masse as the end-all-be-all metric, it's in your interests as a marketer to get less important websites to link to you since they're obviously easier to get. Conversely, if we say you can only get websites above a domain authority of 60, you'll be missing the vast majority of link opportunities on the internet. That's no good either. With all this in mind, we ended up devising a metric we still use today called Cumulative Domain Authority, where each link you generate doesn't count as just a single link but as an accumulation of domain authority values. If you get CNN *and* Running Remote, you score 62 + 92, in other words, 154. There is no debate or discussion about *how* you hit your number—the number itself is crystal clear and it completely aligns with the goals of the company.

The most important job for a remote-first manager is finding the right metric. Once you find the right metric, you've got your instrumentation to get the company where it needs to go, and the meaning is nonnegotiable.

Which brings us to another key dimension: Every metric is quantitative in measurement, not qualitative. "Write a book that you feel will help people to transition to an asynchronous work style" is not a strong metric. "Writing a book that consistently gets a 4.5 star rating or higher on Amazon" is better. Speaking of which, if you should be so inclined, please go to Amazon and give us a five-star rating—we need your metric power!

A metric in its purest form need never be discussed—it is simply reported. If you need to course correct going forward, so be it, but the data is the data. Every team member in a department needs to be responsible for presenting his or her own metrics and reading the relevant metrics of others each week.

Here's how we tag them: Green means we're doing great, yellow means we may not hit our target, and red means we are not on target. The only metrics worth discussing are red ones. We watch the yellow targets, but they aren't up for discussion—yet.

If there is a corollary issue that's stopping you from achieving your metric, you must bring up that issue, separately and preferably asynchronously, with a request for the help or resources you need to get your metric on track. In other words, let the metric stand alone, separate from excuses and reasons.

A goal is not a metric, but metrics have a direct relationship with goals.

Metrics are the backstory.

For instance, we have a goal in our company of retaining $500 churns (customers who pay us more than $500 a month). It shouldn't be a surprise when they quit.

That's why we never ask if a $500-plus customer has quit or not. If the customer has quit, it's already too late for that question. Quitting is a massively lagging indicator of what caused that person to quit in the first place.

What we need metrically is a regular report on how happy our churns are, whether they are expanding their account consistently, and a few other measures we can use to determine whether a customer is going to quit in a month, a quarter, or a year.

If you're bashing your head against the wall trying to address a goal or a problem with a goal, always go back to a metric you can measure three, six, or twelve months beforehand. If you can change the early metric, you can usually increase the chances of hitting your goal.

As we said, each individual has to have at least one main metric. In our experience, one person can have up to five total, but more than five becomes a chaos of numbers where everything is important and therefore nothing is important.

In addition to weekly reports, it's important for top brass to audit these metrics and ask themselves: *Is this really the most important thing we need to talk about inside this business, department, or team? Can two existing metrics be combined to produce a single, stronger indicator? Are there any vanity metrics measuring things we don't really care about?*

As we've said, each metric must be quantitative, with a significant chance for failure. If you can't demarcate success or failure, then there is no point in having that metric. Making people "feel good about their numbers" is not how you build a hyper-growth company.

It's important to schedule a weekly time to report metrics, so that synchronous synergies can be exposed. Some metrics depend on other metrics and you need to have those dependencies tracked. For us to generate leads to the website, the website obviously needs to be up and running—it's not the fault of the marketing department if they don't have a place to send their customers.

A well-reported metric effectively makes finger pointing redundant, as it's clear from the data who or what is or is not executing properly.

There's a deeper dimension to all this metricizing than first meets the eye.

Our program of simple, accurate metric reporting gives everyone in the company the same operational advantage as the CEO (see figure 3).

In fact, strong, shared metrics often give each individual team member a better view of the business than the average CEO, and that view leads to powerful adjustments in participation. If you want your employees to think like an owner, you need to give them the information they need to actually pull it off.

Here's the thing: Good metrics don't happen by chance, and, as we've pointed out, there's really no way to talk your way out of bad metrics. This high-level clarity quickly divides the wheat from the chaff and bypasses the bad mix of vanity, charisma, and bruised feelings that make in-person office work ambiguous.

QUARTERLY SCORECARD

	Responsible	Metric	OCT '21	NOVEMBER 2021				DEC '21	Q4 Totals
			Actuals	Actuals	Forecast	Difference	Target	Actuals	
Business KPI	Michael	MRR from Self-Serve							
		MRR from Inbound Sales-Led							
		MRR from Outbound Sales Led							
		Expansion MRR							
		Contraction MRR							
		Churn MRR							
		Net MRR							
Leads In	Letitia	Website Visitors							
		Inbound SALs							
	Manny	Inbound SQLs							
		Channel SQLs							
		Expansion SQLs							
Revenue	Juan	Self-Serve New Business MRR							
		Self-Serve Net MRR							
	Manny	Inbound MRR							
		Outbound MRR							
		Channel MRR							
	Nicole	Tier 1/2 Expansion MRR							
		Tier 1/2 Contraction MRR							
		Tier 1/2 Churn MRR							
	Juan	SS Expansion MRR							
		SS Contraction MRR							

FIGURE 3

You no longer have to sit in monotonous and sometimes treacherous synchronous meetings, since your entire dashboard is available at all times, updated weekly at worst and instantly at best.

You only need to zero in on those metrics that aren't going well—the ultimate "cut to the chase" time-saver.

Best of all, you can very clearly map out what's driving the business forward and what isn't. When you reconcile your metrics to the P&L (profit and loss statement), positive and negative forces become crystal clear in an instant.

By opening up everyone's metrics company-wide, two important reinforcements take place: First, all employees recognize that they are respected enough to be trusted with the global view. Second, all employees understand that, despite this global view, only one level is 100 percent their responsibility.

This one-two punch is the essence of async empowerment.

ASYNC METRIC DASHBOARDS: THE DARK SIDE

If you implement metric instrumentation into your business, it's amazing what follows. Work gets done and gets reported on, and course correction takes place instantaneously, often without your direct involvement. But the fact is, there are also challenges to a fully async metric system.

These challenges need to be addressed and monitored to ensure the success of your organization:

- **The Silo Trap:** Without a clear recognition of how certain metrics interrelate, you can encounter the dreaded siloing of your business. Siloing is the result of improper async communication. If departments don't deliberately communicate their actions, they have an uncanny habit of duplicating tasks. Metrics don't communicate it all by themselves. You need to identify and bring up issues, interrelationships, and dependencies as quickly as possible, ideally communicated company-wide, asynchronously, leaving a historic record. In short, the whole company needs to know what the whole company is up to. (We love Gantt charts for this, because they literally keep everyone on the same page.)

- **The Unquantifiable Types:** You will meet a lot of artistic individuals who will tell you that you can't measure the results of collaboration, ingenuity, imagination, or poetic inspiration. The simple fact is that even though artistry is harder to measure, that doesn't make it unmeasurable. It's all about choosing the right metrics as they relate to your business. Be creative in the application of metrics and don't be afraid to change them if they're not right, but never leave a core function of your business up to chance. A writer wants to write more "thought leadership" blogs? Measure how often those blogs are shared versus other blogs. Nobody gets to take blind shots in the dark.
- **The Revisionist History Rogues:** These are the worst kind of employees you'll encounter in a fully metrics-based environment. "I didn't really think that this metric was the right one! You forced me to accept this metric, and I wasn't comfortable committing to it!" Wrong. Always encourage your team members to speak up when you introduce metrics. Make them commit to the measure. If they don't think they can hit it, they better speak up. Generally if an employee is off by more than 30 percent, there is a

problem—either with the person or the metric. If the metric is right (which it usually is), it's unfortunately the person. Don't get pulled into the black hole of constantly changing metrics just because they're not fitting one worker's current version of reality.

- **High-Definition Experiments:** Finding the right metric is most of the battle. A properly defined metric that really approaches the root of the goal you're trying to get to will provide clarity and opportunity to experiment against that metric as early as possible. You want to deploy experiments as quickly and as cheaply as possible, and you need a good basis to test them against. The metric is that basis.
- **Vanity Metrics:** There are always numbers that will make your team members feel good, but that don't tell the whole story. If traffic to the website was the ultimate measure for success in our business, we'd only get links from cheap and easy places—but that doesn't translate into actual business. Making people feel good about their work is critical to your company's success, but not if it puts everyone in a false sense of security.

Dan Martell, Remote Pioneer: Buy It Back

"In a distributed team, you can't physically see the quote-unquote manufacturing line, right? Yet you need to have the optics to allow yourself the ability to manage thousands of people remotely."

If there's one person on the planet who understands the power of clarity, it's Dan Martell, legendary SaaS (Software as a Service) coach, the award-winning entrepreneur and investor who founded the Clarity platform—a place for up-and-coming founders and entrepreneurs to receive expert advice. We've known Dan for more than a decade—the world of Canadian tech is a tight-knit one.

Liam can remember having coffee with him years ago and Dan admitting quietly that he was doing a "bit of coaching" for tech founders. Coaching is a bit of a taboo subject in the tech world. There is an unfounded attitude that those who can't do, teach, but with so many years of real experience under his belt, Dan was the only guy who could take us to the next level in our business. We immediately signed on.

Believe us when we say that Dan Martell is not a feel-good coach—he pulls zero punches. In our first meeting, he went straight for our metrics like a pit bull, soundly tearing them to shreds. When he was done, he made his warning clear: Fix your system of measurement, or there is no point in even trying to help you.

In response, we whined. "But what about our Facebook ads? We're not getting the results we'd hoped for. It just didn't work out—"

Dan scoffed. "What's your definition of 'didn't work'? You haven't shown me your numbers, Telling me it 'didn't work' doesn't work for me, and it shouldn't for you either."

Our metrics-consciousness was raised overnight.

After that meeting, we rebuilt our company on a foundation of sturdy measures and regular reporting so that, at any time, we could convey to anyone whether we were succeeding or failing and why.

Today, Dan Martell is really more than a coach or investor, he's a thought leader, with a heavy schedule of speaking engagements. For companies far and wide, Dan Martell is a guru of growth acceleration. Dan's wife jokes that his love language is "being more efficient," but like all jokes, there's some truth in there—he lights up when the conversation turns to improving metrics.

"As a coach, I just help people get clarity around outcomes and achievement," he recently told us, "and metrics are the feedback loop that's required to improve. Whether I'm training for an Ironman [Triathlon] or trying to increase revenue in my business, if I don't have a way to measure efficiency, I can't create a feedback loop, and without a feedback loop, there's no progress."

From our very first meetings, Dan's basic philosophy of metrics has not wavered—and the Async Mindset is something he's been way ahead of the curve on from day one. "Every company is async," he recently told us, "whether they're optimized for it or not. When everybody's walking around with their laptop, or their work device in their back pocket, they need to be able to move things forward without requiring physical presence."

Dan sees an overarching evolution taking place, from qualitative to quantitative analysis. It's an evolution first birthed in engineering and the scientific method, but today, it's influencing businesses, manufacturing, services, and people-driven agencies. In fact, even customer satisfaction—once an amorphous concept debated at length in endless meetings—has been taken over by numbered ratings—specific data to which managers can be held accountable.

"Software really pioneered the whole idea of a metric for happiness," Dan explains. "HubSpot calls it the CHI, the Customer Happiness Index, and it's designed on a bunch of different things that customers may be doing inside the product. That number tells product managers and salespeople if they're building and selling the right stuff. Because if someone buys the product hoping it does X, but in fact it does Y, then the CHI starts to go down."

For Dan, strong metrics have the power to expose where the real opportunities for hyper-growth lie within any given business. He notes, however, that the parameters of a truly strong metric require deep thinking about all the steps—the inputs, outputs, and throughputs that connect every process. Only when the processes are measured in tandem do you have the opportunity to fix weak links and fortify where needed.

"In a distributed team," he says, "you can't physically see the quote-unquote manufacturing line, right? Yet you need to have the optics to allow yourself the ability to manage thousands of people remotely."

Metrics are the heart and soul of those optics.

Dan says that every business requires a core operating system with the ability to measure—what he calls a "precision scorecard"—with three to five critical numbers that will give managers an indicator of the health of their particular department. This precision scorecard, however, is not the most important metric.

"Every company needs what Sean Ellis calls a North Star metric," he says, "that one number that will tell us not only whether we're growing but whether our customers are receiving greater and greater value from us."

Airbnb, for instance, uses "nights booked" as its North Star—a focus point that accretes all the organization's goals into one super-goal. Facebook measures how many customers get seven friends to connect. Our own company tracks time. What's important to note is that, for all of our companies and for yours, too, revenue alone cannot be the North Star metric, because it fails to account for the deeper evolution at work:

repeat usage, user experience, and, ultimately, customer retention.

Dan adds, "I always ask every business: What is a five-star customer for you? And what is it that you do that you monetize? What percentage of your customers were active today versus thirty days ago? **Between engagement and monetization, you can discover your North Star metric.**"

Often, finding the North Star is a matter of identifying the sweet spot, the place where the least amount of effort will engender the greatest retention and highest customer satisfaction. Dan calls the avoidance of this sweet spot "the Goldilocks effect," because companies are usually doing too much or too little to get their customers hooked.

Dan takes some of his greatest lessons from outside the tech world, where engagement and retention can come in all shapes and sizes. For instance, there's what Jon Taffer calls the Red Napkin Strategy: The waiter asks if it's your first visit to that restaurant. If you say yes, he or she switches out your napkin with a red one. Now, the manager and the entire waitstaff know they are making a first impression. And at the end of the night? The last waiter to pick up your bill asks, "What did you have for dessert? The cheesecake? Next time try the crème brûlée—on me."

And when you come back a second time, they reinforce with another offer: ribs gratis on your next visit.

If these gestures seem a little grand, keep in mind the metrics: In a business where 2.4 visits usually lead to nonstop customer retention, you have just greatly upped your chances for that third magical visit that turns you into a die-hard fan.

"To me, that's what I'm always looking for," Dan says. "What's the minimum effective dose? What's the least amount of moving parts that's going to get the biggest bang for our buck?"

It should go without saying that, these days, technology allows for a ridiculous number of ways to track customer behavior. Heat map routers can tell what sections in a store are more populated, and how long each person stays. If you're a store owner and you think metrics like this aren't for you, you're dead wrong.

Often, it's the inside of the remote organization rather than the customer that can be unwieldy. Some employees are more reluctant to be quantified than others, especially engineers and other creative types who tend to problem-solve outside the normal zone of "efficiency." For each and every member of the organization, how do you identify which metrics you actually want to measure versus how they want to be measured?

Dan says that it's a delicate process, because objectives and key results that change a lot or don't change enough can give false impressions. These impressions will either create the wrong kind of excitement or leave employees unnecessarily demoralized.

The motion itself needs to be understood:

- How can we tie this number to the real world?
- What are the activities that lead this number to go up or down?
- What activities precipitate the greatest turbulence?

And finally, the question of all metric questions: Which of these numbers is measuring a real value, and which are mere vanity metrics?

For instance, Dan notes that the number of Instagram followers or the amount of website traffic rarely correlates directly enough to revenue to be held accountable, and without that correlation, the number has no solid function.

"You've got to find the ratio," he explains. "Tie a vanity metric to a productivity metric. Then let's see what the number actually does."

Let's say your Instagram account drives chats, and those chats drive pipeline, and the pipeline generates sales. If your marketing team tells you to grow the Instagram account from fifty thousand to a hundred thousand, your response must be: "But will I get more chats?" Because the chats are the next viable step leading to the opportunities that might actually lead to sales.

Without connecting Instagram followers to chats, you only have a vanity metric.

Dan is adamant about seeing processes in interrelated steps before jumping to conclusions about numbers—from beginning to end, with every beat accounted for.

In fact, he says that metrics are best established in the building process. Without a baseline—which he refers to as *control*—there's no way to test for growth, let alone hyper-growth. Once the control is in place, however, tests may beat the control. Then the test numbers become the new control, and the sky's the limit.

"The worst thing somebody can do," Dan says, "is change seven things and get a positive result . . . but not know what thing they changed made the result. Because then they're going to make an assumption based on all seven things and place an even bigger bet on the thing that might not have been *the* thing." He shakes his head forbiddingly. "Until you measure, you're just playing a game of Whac-A-Mole."

Shane Mac, Remote Pioneer: The Big Mac

> "It's a massive paradigm shift where activity takes precedence over identity, and the implications are mind-expanding."

In the wild world of crypto, Shane Mac is a pioneer's pioneer. As cofounder and president of XMTP.com, he is at the forefront of a whole new communication protocol that just might change the thing we call the Web from the inside out. Just as remote companies are able to distribute work that can be hired from anywhere and assemble companies out of the ether, blockchain technology further extends this mutability with the distribution of value.

In a nutshell, blockchain technology distributes value without having a third party to authenticate that value. You can buy a house using blockchain to contract, and you won't need a lawyer to authenticate buyer or seller. It's an openness that is strikingly similar to the Async Mindset in remote-first organizations, where the distribution of work is authenticated, measured, and managed through the processes and platforms we've discussed in this book.

We met Shane at a tech conference in 2011. At the time, he was the product manager for a company called Zaarly, which had just raised more than $15 million and was quickly becoming the darling of the tech world. The app was designed to help users enter the next evolution of the sharing economy by allowing them to monetize quite literally *anything*—you could even borrow someone's phone charger for an hour, stick it up on the platform, and give it a value for trading. Ever need a charger in a busy coffee shop? The idea was magnificent. If everyone was on Zaarly, you'd be able to go two seats over and borrow a charger for a buck.

In the ten years that followed, we couldn't help but notice that every time we spoke with Shane, he was thinking ten years ahead of everybody else. Way back in the dark ages of 2011, he was already sure that everyone would eventually work remotely and not because it was "easier for workers" but because it was a better way of extracting value from labor. He simply saw the remote explosion as an inevitability. It wasn't too long before he was proven right. By 2019, Shane started a fund for remote teams that has ended up being one of the top performers in the industry. It would be an understatement to say he's got his finger on the pulse.

Although we have stated in this book that charisma is not a requirement for the new remote normal, Shane is that rare guy who just instinctively knows how to work the room—in fact, it's a key part of his wide vision. One night in Florida, we dared to ask him what kind of trouble we should get ourselves into and ended up first in the hottest club on Miami Beach, then on a mega yacht, and finally up in one of the most luxurious penthouses in the city, partying the night away. Making connections is incredibly easy for Shane—unlike us! So, it's no surprise that his personal and professional mission is about connecting people.

"Since I was young, I was just always curious," he recently told us. "Curious about bringing together people that were disconnected." In 2005, when he discovered Facebook and Twitter like the rest of us, Shane instantly embraced the widened scope as few had. He realized that he could talk to anybody on the planet, literally anyone. He sent out his first tweet, back in the days when a tweet was a mere SMS. "I was getting responses from these random SMS numbers, and I was like—'I just said something to the world!'"

The realization that there was a chasm between online and offline identities was something Shane began to grasp at a very deep level. Attending state college in Macomb, Illinois, population eight thousand, he started moonlighting as a wedding singer and at happy hour bars for $30 on a Friday night. Often audience members would pull him aside and ask him to perform at their weddings—big, solid $3,000 gigs. He'd never done weddings before, so he made an iTunes playlist and sang a few numbers between the hits, and people loved it. For one year, Shane was a surprisingly successful one-man band.

One day, while contacting wedding photographers, Shane began to experiment with his emails. "I built this little script that would scrape the email address, look up on Facebook and MySpace and Twitter, and then put a little photo in the email. And it sounds so dumb and basic, but I saw it as something that just helped me have more of a connection to who I was talking to."

When he moved to Nashville, however, he got a better view of the competition. After seeing the nth incredible singer in a row there, he said, "Maybe I shouldn't sing anymore."

He began to explore the world of messaging and texts, and ways it could disrupt "the website as a billboard," making way for a two-way interface with customers. "It starts with language and communication," Shane insists. "There's a reason why they have ten thousand people programming Alexa to be empathetic, so that even when she's not right, you love her."

Even now, years later as a true maverick in the world of Web 3.0, Shane understands as few do that these machines are only as useful as the connections they foster. "What's going to happen in a world where crypto wallets need to talk to each other?" he asks. "The last Web was about identity over activity. You start out with who is Person X, I will message Person X."

The next wave of internet life, as Shane explains it, is going to have a decidedly different tack. "You'll start with what do they do, what do they own, what are they working on? Then I'll send them a message and find out who they are."

It's a massive paradigm shift where activity takes precedence over identity, and the implications are mind-expanding. When what you do and what you're working on have primacy over who you are, what your status is, where you come from, or where you went to school, you have essentially entered a vanity-free meritocracy that runs on metrics.

This deep, almost philosophical understanding about the way we use data may be why Shane's thoughts on metrics are counterintuitive and unique. "Metrics to me are less about the number, and more important about accountability," he says. "The metrics themselves can always change, but your self-awareness and your attention to them are what count."

This philosophy of metric accountability isn't just an idea—he practices it every day. To cite just one example, his personal trainer follows up to track his exercise regimen—every day. Shane says, "I'm really, really bad at being accountable to myself. And that's the problem with metrics, if you're by yourself, it's really hard to be accountable. For me, I never want to let someone else down. That's what drives me."

As Shane explains it, metrics must be perceived as "the outcome of assumptions," and they're only as good as the testing they do or don't bear out. "Did whatever assumption you made about the future happen or not?" he asks. "Either way, be honest and it's fine. If it didn't, it's either because you weren't good at it or you were wrong about your assumptions. *Or* maybe your assumption did happen and let's try to do more."

Like Dan Martell and so many remote pioneers, Shane is an efficiency nut whose lifestyle itself is a reflection of metricized values. He literally lives by a reminder engine that pokes him about what to do and when to do it. He won't do meetings or schedule anything before 11:00 a.m., because he finds the early hours are best for deep, unscripted work—a realization that came from noticing that his most impactful day was usually Saturday. He also insists on not being the CEO of any of his ventures, because it allows him to better face the most taboo subjects about any given company—its burn rate, its weak spots, its fate. He has assigned himself the role of "man behind the curtain."

But of all Shane's metricized habits, the one we love best is something we'll call "ten people every day for ten years." It's a simple extension of that very first SMS he sent out years ago.

Every single day, Shane reaches out to ten people *just because.* "If you're helpful to people by actually reaching out—about ways to get feedback on their product or by knowing they're in the news and asking questions about them that are specific to what they've been working on, because you're genuinely curious—you can build relationships and start conversations with anyone in the world."

Twelve years after starting this habit, he still blocks off one hour every single day. Using a contact management tool called Clay, in which he has invested, he spends time thinking of the people he hasn't spoken with recently, reading about everyone, trying to come up with a useful reason to reach out, be helpful, or just build a connection. Ten people a day, 365 days a year, twelve years—that's almost forty-five thousand people . . . so far.

Often, Shane is asked if it's worth it, all this effort, all this contact. He is adamant that that is the wrong question, askers are missing the point. "If you can be helpful to ten people a day? Everything in your life will happen! It's one of those things where you have to believe in long-term karma while practicing short-term metrics."

He's also refreshingly honest about the selfish component in all this. In order to help others, he is compelled to use their products, give feedback, and learn things along the way. Another key aspect to Shane's "ten a day" rule is that he's tracking activity, not outcome, in order to reinforce the right behaviors for his business.

There is a subtle way that Shane's activities upend internet sociability the way it's most commonly understood. Instead of worrying about how big his network is, he focuses on how helpful he can be. "That's the metric I track to run my life—how many people say 'thank you.'"

REMOTE METRIC FUNDAMENTALS

Often, the greatest challenge in the art of metrics is not acquiring the numbers, but knowing how to use them to discover the true state of things. According to business.com's Isaac Kohen, data is the "abundant resource" of our new age and "many organizations are surrounded by oceans of information." For smaller teams without the training and know-how, data analysis is an uphill battle.

Kohen prescribes five simple metrics that are as stable as the four major food groups—you can't survive without understanding them: 1) engagement, 2) productivity, 3) efficiency, 4) well-being, and 5) future-casting.

Engagement is not a matter of "more is better." Kohen describes it as a valuable metric that can "cut both ways." Longer work hours paradoxically can correlate to lower productivity (and long-term burnout).

Productivity means tracking actions—everything from mouse activity to app engagement to email quantity and beyond. The key, as Kohen describes it, is making sure productivity impacts profitability.

Efficiency includes everything from process standardization to streamlining communication methodologies and scheduling best practices. According to Kohen, even behemoths like Microsoft "have made transformative changes to their operations to maximize efficiency for a hybrid workforce," optimizing its meeting schedule to avoid peak productivity hours.

Well-being is more than a clean bill of health. Sleep difficulties, substance abuse, chronic worry, and feelings of isolation can all be exacerbated by remote-first work when they aren't counterbalanced with healthy habits and human contact.

Finally, *future-casting* is the rock-bottom use of good metrics, so that "everyday business owners can chart new goals for organizational structures, collaborative teams, and outcomes-focused hiring."[1]

Kenjo[2] blog smartly points out that SMART objectives—that is, objectives that are Specific, Measurable, Achievable, Relevant, and Timely—must always be "well-defined and fulfill specific requirements." To illustrate, they hunker down on a specific for each letter of the acronym:

- **Specific:** increase visitors to our website
- **Measurable:** 30 percent more visits
- **Achievable:** doubling our content
- **Relevant:** to launch a campaign
- **Timely:** in one month

CHAPTER 4 TAKEAWAYS

1. Only vivid and specific metrics have the power to set remote workers free to do what they do best. Counterintuitively, the more you measure, the more freedom you have.
2. Metrics are crucial for self-management at the top. Achieving flow state requires taking stock of minute reporting so you and your company can focus on what's important.
3. In addition, top brass always needs to assess if the most important aspects of the business are being measured. They also need to know that information is available to everyone, so everyone can think like an owner.
4. Some of the most successful, fastest-growing, remote companies are run by introverted types who keep their focus on the numbers instead of their egos.
5. Most old-school companies don't really have metrics, they have tertiary data that is "about metrics." If the person assigned to the number can't move it, it's not a metric.
6. In a remote-first, async company, all the members of the team have a number they report on weekly, with an intended target and a significant chance of failure.
7. Often, the best metrics describe a relationship between activities rather than a single process. In addition, two existing metrics can often be

combined to produce a single, stronger indicator. When possible, combine and reduce metrics, and remove those that aren't relevant.

8. A well-defined and well-reported metric makes finger pointing senseless and redundant, since it will be clear from the data who is delivering and who isn't.
9. By the same token, you can't talk your way out of bad metrics.
10. Every company needs a North Star metric that guides the whole operation. Start with the most important number in your business that directly produces value in the shortest amount of time. Most would think that it's money, but in most cases it's something smarter like time tracked.
11. Metrics serve two key functions, each equally important: First, they obviously measure what needs to be measured. Second, they keep human beings accountable.
12. On a related note, metrics are just as useful for tracking activity as they are for tracking outcome.
13. When formulating new metrics, consider the basic foundations: engagement, productivity, efficiency, well-being, and future-casting.

PART II

The Timeless Team: Building Remote/ Async Culture

FIVE
The End of Cities

To be sure, the Async Mindset is not just a technical matter, or even just a work matter. In a development that nobody could have predicted even twenty years ago, the network of collaboration and company culture has moved into a totally digital realm, and the implications for cities—especially tech hubs like Silicon Valley, New York, Toronto, and Austin—are enormous.

Just why do we hang on to the primacy of the city office anyway? We'll look to evolutionary biology for an answer.

In evolution, there are plenty of changes that don't really spell maximum success. Take the recurrent laryngeal nerve,[1] running from the brainstem, looping through the aortic arch and coming back to the larynx. (We swear this is not turning into a biology textbook, just bear with us.) The nerve is present in all mammals. You may not know it but you probably use it every waking minute of your life. So far, so good, right?

Well, not for giraffes.

In a giraffe's neck, the laryngeal nerve is almost fifteen feet long. Seriously—it's hilariously inefficient. It's not *hurting* the giraffe per se, but it's an incredibly stupid design considering that, functionally, it could be a mere six inches long if it didn't loop through the heart.

In the world of business, the push for innovation is constant—in products, in services, in brands and styles . . . but ironically, *not in work itself*. Most companies operate on a series of basic evolutionary assumptions so invisible to the naked eye that we take them for granted. These are the laryngeal nerves of your organization—complex, overwrought, and totally unnecessary.

The good news is, unlike a giraffe, your company's processes can be rerouted. The bad news is, to fix them, you've got to identify them first.

For all its great strides and advances, Silicon Valley's business model is fundamentally flawed, in no small part because it is highly dependent upon a series of *homogenizations*: venture capital funding, uniform culture, top-down thinking, and the never-ending yearning for a big exit. This deadly combo sets the tone.

Like a lot of tech companies who want to "make it" in the eyes of the tech elite, we've tried to raise venture capital funds at a variety of stages, with varying results. Our own experiences interfacing with VC funds have been eye-opening, to say the least.

Just a few years in, we had invested plenty of cash and sweat equity, and even though we weren't drawing salaries yet, we knew we had a good-enough growth rate—any venture capitalist would love to at least consider us for their portfolio. Liam, being the less awkward of the two of us, went hunting for VCs. (Although, since we were already making a profit, we had no idea what we would actually *do* with VC money should we get some, but that didn't matter.) Our approach was typical for young start-ups: "Raising money will make us seem important."

We spoke to a few dozen VCs and got a lot of predictable feedback: "You've built an impressive business. Let's stay in touch."

Which, of course, is a nice way of saying, "Don't call us, we'll call you."

We did, however, get a few term sheets, which in effect are soft offers to invest in your business. The conversation around those term sheets usually went something like this:

"Hey, Rob and Liam, we love your business, and what you've built up until this point, and we love the whole remote angle, we think it's very synergistic to our portfolio."

Translation: *"We can sell you for a good multiple to our partners."*

"We also love the amount of dry powder (unallocated funds you have in the business), and once we finish up our due diligence, we'd love to offer you millions of dollars in capital."

Translation: *"We need to make sure you aren't just two weirdos from the internet."*

"But, just one thing. Before we tie all this up, one minor sticking point. . . . Er, um, er . . . Where you're located. Rob's in Australia, Liam's in Canada, engineering and vice presidents are all over the place. What we'd really love is if you could just bring everyone to one place. In fact, why not relocate to our city?"

Yeah. No.

Each firm wanted us to move the whole operation—to San Francisco, Toronto, Montreal, or New York—wherever *they* were located, "to build a synergistic company culture, which is so critical to really achieving hyper-growth."

To which we responded by scratching our heads. "So, let us get this straight. You want our company—whose mission statement is to help transition the world toward remote work—to move everyone to one city? Don't you think our customers would find that hypocritical?"

"No, no! Don't get us wrong, we love the remote work angle! We think it's a great hook. But trust us, we're VCs and we know how to build tech unicorns, and the only way to really make that happen is when you're all under one roof."

To make a long story short, we didn't take the money, not because we didn't want it, but because it simply went against the core values of our company. You can't build remote under one roof.

Here's the punchline: Fast-forward ten years, and half of those VCs are now tripping over themselves, investing in remote-first companies. They finally discovered that, yes, you really can build and scale a business *not* under one roof. A few of those VC firms have actually called us asking for our help. Would we be willing to talk to their teams about how to measure and manage a remote-first company? Despite the huge chip on our shoulders, we've always said yes, because, hey, it's our mission.

Keep in mind—the VCs didn't embrace the Async Mindset because it finally seemed fun to them. They learned that it is very quickly becoming the only viable model for what they love most—hyper-growth.

IN THE LAND OF FALSE ASSUMPTIONS

There are a zillion reasons people trained by the Silicon Valley model are resistant toward remote work. Here are just a few:

- **Management by Presence:** Some people think that if employees are *there,* that means they're working. But just showing up doesn't mean you're actually doing anything useful at all. Research shows that businesses lose $600 billion a year to workplace distractions, and that remote workers are 35 to 40 percent more productive than their in-office counterparts. Among performance-based remote work statistics in 2020, 94 percent of surveyed employers report that company productivity has been the same (67 percent) or higher (27 percent) since employees started working from home during the pandemic. In fact, in a FlexJobs[2] survey of more than 2,100 people who worked remotely during the pandemic, it was found that 51 percent report being more productive working from home, and 95 percent say productivity has been higher or the same while working remotely.

  According to Bloomberg,[3] the work-from-home boom will ultimately lift productivity in the US economy by 5 percent, mostly because of savings in commuting time. The findings suggest the rapid adoption of new technology amid the pandemic will offer lasting economic gains, helping to boost sluggish productivity that has long weighed on global growth.
- **The False Assumption of Concentration of Labor:** It might have once been true that you'd find the best people in San Francisco or New York City, but no more. As the very highest-level talent leaves the big cities, the new

concentration of labor is in a place less easily defined—anywhere and everywhere. That's why learning to acquire talent remotely—which we cover in chapter 6—is so crucial a survival skill.

- **The False Assumption of Plentiful Labor:** For the first time in US history, there are more people leaving the workforce than entering it. Labor will continue to go up in price, not just in the Western world but everywhere, and going into international markets is quickly becoming the only way to hedge against the increase in costs. During the pandemic, our own engineering talent went up nearly 25 percent for new hires, simply because large tech companies were allowing their engineers to go remote.

  Several studies of the Silicon Valley exodus demonstrate the idea that no city is safe from labor loss, but consider the following: Remote work never loses labor due to migration. As Techmonitor describes it, "Before the pandemic, the Bay Area was already experiencing a net outflow of residents. . . . The pandemic has accelerated what was already an emerging trend in the area: exorbitantly high rents, combined with the increased possibilities for remote work, leading many tech workers to seek more space in more affordable areas. . . . Among the most common reasons for moving were improving their home environment and a lower cost of living."[4]
- **The False Assumption that Remote Management and Collaboration Don't Mix:** As we've explained, old-school synchronous management just doesn't work remotely. The Async Mindset is not only easier to execute but more efficient, creating a more efficient and competitive model. It's not that remote hinders management and collaboration, it's that stale modes don't take hold remotely.

- **The Cult of Personality:** Without a doubt, a big office feeds a big ego, and when you are surrounded by a lot of people who do whatever you tell them to do, it's almost impossible to not make vanity your North Star metric. By contrast, top brass in remote-first organizations are rarely flashy.

In fact, the Async Mindset creates a culture that eschews ostentatiousness or obnoxiousness of any kind. You can't show off when you have nobody to show off to.

In one coworking space that we sometimes worked at, a person we'll lovingly refer to as Start-up Karen was the bane of our day. She liked to boss her colleagues around, yell through loud sales calls, and dress down fellow employees for not working hard enough without ever setting any quantifiable goals for them.

One day, in the middle of a tirade, she said, "We should start to work with more important tech start-ups in town like Shopify or Time Doctor!"

Her employee gently pointed out that the founders of Time Doctor—in other words, us—were sitting in the next cubicle.

What's especially poignant about this story is that Start-up Karen had worked next to us in the coworking space for more than a year and hadn't taken the time to ask our names, where we came from, or what we were doing. All she saw were a couple of tech nerds—enough to write us off. On the scale of vanity metrics, we didn't rate. We had no big flashy office, we had no yes men or women around us. We just did the work that produced a company at least ten times bigger than hers in the same amount of time, growing the business through asynchronous collaboration and quantifiable metrics, not through free jelly beans or having a slide in our office.

Don't get us wrong, the slides are fun, but hyper-growth is more fun.

EPIC SILICON VALLEY FAILS

We aren't the only ones who've become disillusioned with the great promises of start-up culture in Silicon Valley. As Aytekin Tank recently wrote in Jotform,[5] Silicon Valley started out looking like the "better-looking, more humane alternative to banks and multinationals . . . the Robin Hood of business."

Today, however, Tank asserts that the area has lost its moral high ground, with less than 5 percent of ideas that receive funding coming from women, and less than 1 percent of venture money going to African Americans and Latinos. For a culture that once distinctly vowed to foster diversity and equality, those are some ghastly numbers, exacerbated by regular headlines about sexual harassment and employee abuse.

The bloom is off the SV rose, but nowhere is its image more tarnished than in the realm of data privacy. *Financial Times*[6] and *Vanity Fair*[7] predict a wide-sweeping backlash as the world faces what some describe as a "dire privacy crisis" as new ePrivacy laws struggle to come into place.

As Tank puts it, "The data manipulation offenses Silicon Valley commits every day are so widespread we barely even notice them anymore."

Finally, the SV business culture itself, which engenders fraud by encouraging start-ups to fake it till they make it. Leveraging legal loopholes and reporting outright inaccurate or misleading information in the name of getting venture traction have hit an ugly saturation point. According to Tank, in SV, the truth has become optional.

The way we see it, none of this is accidental. At least part of the problem stems from the simple fact that Silicon Valley is not remote.

What that means is that the people who made the place what it is can't help but suffer from a kind of hermetically sealed homogeny. That very homogeny is the kryptonite that tints what a decision maker can see, think, and act.

Or, to put it in layman's terms, the residents of SV think they own the place—and don't wanna share.

Of course, big money plays its part. Silicon Valley is not merely an industrial zone, it's a peculiar one-of-a-kind wealth bubble where employees can draw six-figure salaries yet struggle to cover sky-high rents and Bay Area lifestyles. As the *Guardian* puts it, "The prohibitive costs have displaced teachers, city workers, firefighters and other members of the middle class, not to mention low-income residents."[8]

Somewhere along the way, Silicon Valley and reality got a divorce.

To cite just one atrocious example, take a look at Zenefits—the first privately held SV unicorn to be penalized by the SEC. As Jay Rao reports for Quartz at Work, Zenefits had all the hallmarks of Silicon Valley Gone Wrong—"a frat house atmosphere, a fixation on stratospheric growth, and a willingness to play fast and loose with regulations."[9]

Zenefits is not the only such company coming under scrutiny. Diagnostic testing company Theranos was also penalized for lying to investors, and Uber recently settled a $10 million discrimination lawsuit after widespread accusations of sexual harassment, pay discrimination, and a hostile work environment.

Zenefits, however, serves as the strongest example, because its atmosphere was toxic and its fall was steep.

Rao defines six interconnected building blocks to help frame what we mean when we say "company culture"—resources, processes, success, values, behaviors, and climate or "the quality and tenor of workplace life." For our purposes, it's interesting to note how deeply all six aspects are affected by being a remote-first company. That's why it's near impossible to imagine a company like Zenefits thriving remotely.

As Rao tells it, Zenefits founder and CEO Parker Conrad set the stage for a frenetic work atmosphere with a hard-hitting sales force that played as rough as they worked. Their motto—"Ready, Fire, Aim!"—was not merely a wisecrack. They made a habit of lying to potential clients, dodging insurance regulations, and valuing growth over every other indicator of company health.

In particular, Zenefits did not set up the *processes* required to mature—the arduous but absolutely nonnegotiable task we describe in chapter 3.

Here's what happens when you skirt that step: In 2015 the company started coming apart at the seams. By early 2016, high-level executives started to resign. Subsequently 17 percent of the workforce was laid off and the enterprise team was closed. By September 2017, Zenefits changed its business model from an insurance broker to a SaaS platform for brokers, offering human resources, payroll, benefits, and wellness applications for small businesses.

Oh, they also changed their motto—from "Ready, Fire, Aim!" to "Operate with Integrity."

We wish them luck.

DON'T START UP

It's long been our contention that it's better to run a business than a start-up. A start-up is a rocket headed heaven-knows-where; it's focused on growth at all costs, and even profits are secondary to getting your next round of financing. A business is something that grows, producing value for its customers and dividends for its shareholders. Be a sturdy tortoise, not a directionless hare.

For instance, there's a long-held tradition in Silicon Valley: Hire somebody who is 10 percent better for double or triple whatever they're currently making. It's just one more way to pour on the rocket fuel at all costs because, again, the goal isn't profit and sustainability but acquisition. This kind of on-ramping can work sometimes for managers or top-shelf engineers, but there is a lot of serious talent out there that would sacrifice money for autonomy and freedom. Throwing cash at the problem is not the solution.

A few years ago, we hired one of the best software developers on planet Earth. That's not hyperbole—this person actually won a top ten finish in the annual Facebook hackathon. He then received a high six-figure offer from Facebook and another super-high offer from Google, but he ended up going with little ole us for way less money, fewer perks, and less prestige. Can you explain it?

Well, we snagged him for one reason and one reason only: freedom. This guy realized that even though we were offering way less money, we were also offering way more flexibility than the behemoths of Silicon Valley that were going to force him into a gilded-cage cubicle, stuff him with free sushi, and send him off to hour-long yoga sessions.

The man in question is not alone. There's a wildly growing segment of the working world ready to earn less money in exchange for greater freedom from space and time constraints. A recent survey from Remote finds that "76 percent of those polled (say) they would accept a salary reduction if they were able to work remotely anywhere in the world." The survey goes on to note that numbers vary worldwide, with US respondents on average willing to accept a slightly higher reduction at 17 percent versus 10 percent for UK respondents, but a whopping 23 percent of respondents believe that embracing remote work will ultimately help reduce salary costs for businesses.[10]

What we're experiencing is not merely a seasonal variance. It's the transformation of a generation of workers who are willing to exchange less pay for greater sanity.

With that in mind, it's our contention that employers will have to wake up to the changes or find themselves adrift. No longer can you attract top talent through expensive lunches or swankier offices.

The Silicon Valley Epoch—with its *Game-of-Thrones*-like power structure—has served its historic purpose. Ultimately, though, it re-entrenched a cultural and economic homogenization that was already in place, and that cul-de-sac is not where history is headed. Diversity and inclusivity—which we'll dive into more deeply in chapter 6—is just a natural fit for remote-first work environments. In fact, "diversity" is too small a word for the mix we support. Our team members come from all continents, all religions, all racial groups, all sexual identities. The crosshatch creates something that is beyond the opposite of homogenization—it's a move toward international egolessness, where proof of work is the only "centrism."

Andreas Klinger, Remote Pioneer: Hyper-growth the UnValley Way

"Silicon Valley in the cloud."

Don't think we're being glib—we know the idea of companies without cities is radical. For this powerful concept to take hold, supports have to be in place. That's where Andreas Klinger comes in.

He leads a fund called Remote First Capital, an elite group of founders, operators, and other smart people betting on the next generation of remote work. Remote First has a twofold agenda—to empower those start-ups that improve remote work, and to empower those start-ups that leverage remote work in a unique way.

In 2018, Liam was hanging out in the back of a house in Miami that Rob picked up during the 2011 real estate collapse. Rob was a bit of a burner in his younger years, and the Miami house was a microcosm of all things Burning Man. When Liam jumped on a Zoom call with Andreas Klinger, he didn't realize that he was standing in front of a two-story, fire-breathing techno alien that Rob had bought during one of his trips to the desert.

Within a few minutes, Andreas said, "What is that thing behind you?"

"Oh, that's just Rob's techno alien, want me to make it shoot a fireball for you?"

"Uh, yes," Andreas said, "I'd love to see that."

This was just the icebreaker we needed. Liam had been pretty nervous about asking Andreas to fly halfway across the planet to the Running Remote conference in Bali, Indonesia. At the time, Andreas was the CTO of Product Hunt, and it had just been acquired by AngelList—serious front-page, start-up news. Product Hunt's unique platform meant that anybody could show up on the internet with a new product or service, and it would be upvoted by the community. If you made it to the top, you'd be exposed to hundreds of thousands of customers flooding your website. It was a brilliant idea, and, in no time, Product Hunt had effectively become kingmakers of the tech world.

We honestly don't know why Andreas took a chance with us. Maybe it was the fireball-shooting techno alien. But in any case, he agreed to speak at our conference. Afterward, at our retreat, he said, sort of thinking out loud, "I wish there was a fund that just invested solely in remote-first companies and tools. There isn't anything like that right now, and if we think remote is going to be as big as we think it is, well. . . ."

Today, that dream is a reality.

Andreas is also responsible for inventing the term "head of remote," a moniker that is cropping up in more and more organizations worldwide. "We actually originally meant 'head of remote products,'" Andreas says with a laugh, "but it sounded weird."

Remote First Capital was born, primarily because Andreas saw so many opportunities in the remote space, yet he was unable to convince VCs to invest. "It was kind of like, 'Okay, f*** it, I'll do it myself.'" RFC has invested in a steady stream of wildly successful companies from Hopin to Remote (remote.com) to Galileo to On Deck, whose handle is "Silicon Valley in the cloud."

To put it mildly, Remote First Capital is doing rather well.

"What the remote pioneers essentially did," Andreas explains, "is they aggregated a lot of the best practices we usually only associate with larger teams. Explicit processes, handbooks, standards, async communication."

Every company needs to switch to these processes as they grow in size. Remote pioneers have been forced to understand these principles a little earlier.

"The big insight that remote teams have," Andreas says, "is that they have earlier explicit needs for processes, but therefore, they also scale a lot easier afterwards."

Andreas is quick to point out that he has nothing against offices per se, but in typical pioneer fashion, he prefers to work in what he calls a "non-headquarter city," in a smaller space, with four or five other nerds, each person "doing their thing."

Through his fundraising efforts, he's observed a change in the general consciousness about offices over the years. At first, investors insisted that the whole team be in one place. Then they softened their position—if the founder and execution team were in one place, everyone else could be anywhere. Finally, investors started to take the big leap toward all-remote.

"For me, there are really two different aspects at play," he explains. "One is 'online work,' and the other is 'global work.'" He says that if remote work simply means working on a laptop and using the internet, then the world is already pretty much remote and has been for some time.

The remaining issue is how global an organization wants to be.

"There are async processes and async time zones," he says, "and a lot of people trip over this differentiation. When most people say *async,* they mean processes—you do A, then B, then C, without micromanagement."

For Andreas, the move toward async time zones, however, presents the real next step in the revolution—a robust leap away from Silicon Valley–centric work life. Andreas posits two axes—time and space, the time zone and the physical hub—that every global company must face. A company can have everyone in the same general time zone with workers who are not physically close to one another, or they can have hubs of teams across multiple time zones, or some combo thereof. The real-life variations are endless, presenting some very definite new challenges.

"How close are you to the next hub?" he asks. "How async can we be? Can we create some kind of interaction, some kind of cultural state out of sync?"

Andreas predicts that future-facing organizations will have to be conscious of these two axes and the way they interrelate if they are going to grow happy teams and functional processes. New distance creates the need for charting new dependencies and new sequences and uncovering new risks.

However, if all this sounds a little portentous, he notes that the move toward global remote-first is all but inevitable. "Every sufficiently large company is a remote team in denial, because they already have the same async processes, and very frequently they also have teams split in different areas."

The word *global* might sound grandiose, but stepping outside Silicon Valley and putting your business in the cloud is simply the most obvious step a company can take to prepare for hyper-growth. If you need to hire fast, if you need to scale horizontally, if you need to 5x or 10x on processes that are already in place, you need to "go out of town"—the planet will always have a talent capacity advantage over your home base. "Even if you're in a Chinese city with twenty million people, there's still more people on the outside."

According to Andreas, the most important thing to prepare for is that the remote-first organization will usually pay their dues in earlier stages. "If all of a sudden you hire twenty more people, and then another forty, and then eighty, you can't turn around and say, *'Nobody wrote the f***ing handbook, nobody had time for it!'*"

The beauty of remote teams is that they think about handbooks and other scalable processes from day one.

"The future of hyper-growth," Andreas says, "*is* remote."

HATERS GONNA HATE

You know an idea is strong when it's got violent detractors tripping over one another to be the first to discredit it.

In August 2021, Rebecca Stropoli wrote in *Chicago Booth Review* that a "persistent sticking point" in the debate about remote work "has been productivity." While some large-scale companies like Facebook and Spotify are leaning into remote-first, "others, such as JPMorgan Chase and Goldman Sachs, are reverting to the tried-and-true office environment, calling everyone back in. Goldman's CEO David Solomon, in February 2021, called working from home an 'aberration that we're going to correct as quickly as possible.' And JPMorgan CEO Jamie Dimon said of exclusively remote work: 'It doesn't work for those who want to hustle. It doesn't work for spontaneous idea generation. It doesn't work for culture.'"[11]

We're grateful that Dimon used this term "hustle," because it cuts to the quick about every falsehood that we believe on-premise work perpetrates. The culture of what has been called "hustle porn," making glamorous those people who are pushiest, loudest, and most glad-handing, in other words, the antithesis of the Async Mindset. As far as we're concerned, hustle is dumb, or, to be more exact, hustle is what naive people look for when they are seeking "the hardworking." Hustle is another word for working hard and not smart.

Even more misguided is a recent remote hit piece from the *Washington Post*'s Edward Glaeser and David Cutler. "Research suggests that a switch to permanent remote work would make us all less productive," Glaeser and Cutler posit without much evidence. "People who shift to working from home can temporarily increase the amount of work they get done in a given day. But over the medium to long term, long-distance employment can't deliver key benefits—including learning and new friendships—that come from face-to-face contact."[12]

After all this bloviated malarkey, they deliver the kicker—a claim for which they have absolutely no hard proof: "In-person work fosters innovation, the effects of which on productivity almost certainly exceed the gains from working harder at home for possibly unsustainable stretches."

What we love most about this piece are the 936 rants in the comments section, jam-packed with people disputing their assertions and railing against their claims:

"Bull."

"Sounds like BS to me."

"Quit being monsters."

"Instead of making a blanket statement like this, which is clearly false, you should be acknowledging that some jobs and employees adapt quite well to working from home . . . ignore that if you dare."

"Sounds like a problem with management, not with the workers working from home."

"We all understand that these two Harvard professors damning you to a life of wage slave servility locked in a hermetically sealed building—while you forgo raising your own children and any semblance of personal life—can work remotely anytime, any day, and from anywhere in the world that they would like to, right?"

Now, tell us the truth: Your best ideas, did they happen in an office meeting?

CHAPTER 5 TAKEAWAYS

1. The new network of collaboration is in the cloud, not Silicon Valley. With remote work, you literally "don't need to go there"—not for people, not for money, not for collaboration. Today, collaboration is digital and distributed. This "netherzone" is everywhere, putting an end to the last in the line of on-premise centers for collaboration like Berlin, London, Istanbul, or Rome.
2. Perks like Ping-Pong tables and nap pods aren't culture or freedom.
3. In fact, the "water cooler culture" is a petri dish for hierarchy, gossip, and office politics.
4. Silicon Valley's business model is fundamentally flawed because it's highly dependent upon a series of homogenizations including venture capital funding, uniform culture, top-down thinking, and the drive for a big exit.
5. In general, people trained in the Silicon Valley model resist remote work, because they believe in archaic modes like management by presence, the false assumption of concentration of labor, the false belief that labor is always plentiful, and the cult of personality that makes stars out of CEOs.

6. Remote async work eschews ostentatiousness or obnoxiousness of any kind.
7. Remote async work also puts its energy into running businesses rather than start-ups. What that means is that the accent is on service, sustainability, and hyper-growth, not giant exits.
8. Remote platforms like project management tools and Zoom rooms are the new office. They are cheaper and easier to spin up and spin down than their on-premise counterparts. Spending half your budget on cool offices and overpriced employees is quickly becoming a thing of the past.
9. Data shows that, for the average person, work-life balance is more important than more money. More employees choose relevance and autonomy in their work over a bigger paycheck. Build your company and culture accordingly.
10. Working for one company for a whole career is increasingly rare. Remote makes switching that much easier.
11. From the employer's perspective, the idea is not to retain employees so much as to move them in and out with greater ease. The Async Mindset puts the power in processes, not "hoarders of sacred knowledge."
12. Initial distribution of capital is more important for tech start-ups, and every dollar you save on office space means more capital to put into real assets that have the potential to produce real growth.

SIX

On-ramping the Remote Worker

Among the many challenges of building and sustaining a remote work environment, none is more pressing than mastering hiring, on-ramping, and nurturing the new employee. Finding new employees and getting them on-board is no longer a job that an entrepreneur can leave in someone else's hands—old-school human resource models have proven ineffective for the kinds of organizations the remote pioneers built.

In fact, it's worth noting that we don't even call our hiring department "human resources," because we don't think humans are mere resources. As remote pioneers, we know that, until you have earned a person's true internal commitment, you haven't even begun to partner.

To draw in the best people, the remote manager or team leader must go past the usual criteria and understand each potential employee's unique life challenges, including time management issues, work-life home split, higher goals, and more.

Paradoxically, it's a process that's a lot more personal than the traditional hiring practice.

A layer of complexity is added to the remote hiring process when we consider the largest factor that makes remote teams unique: They're not only *not* local, they're often global. This means that remote companies are both more scalable and more instantly international.

Multiple nationalities, multiple currencies, multiple time zones, and multiple cultures all on the same team is the new normal.

Of course, it's important to add that a global talent pool means global competition. Remote work makes everyone more replaceable, but by the same token, remote workers have more places to go, and "remote-readiness" is likely to become a rated hiring factor for employers and employees alike.

Here are just a few interesting facts about the way the world of global workers operates:

- At least 65 percent of global workers see remote work as a top company perk.
- According to a TINYpulse report, it's 35 percent faster to hire remote workers than on-site workers.[1]
- According to Review 42, people who work remotely earn $4,000 more per year on average "due to remote, relating to jobs that are in higher demand."[2]
- US companies that allow remote working have a 25 percent lower employee turnover rate, per Owl Labs.[3]
- And last but not least, CNBC reported in October 2020 that an astonishing fourteen to twenty-three

million US workers are planning to move or have moved because of their ability to work remotely.[4]

What those numbers will look like by the time you read this is anybody's guess, but one thing is for sure: The revolution is underway, and it is worldwide.

To put it in perspective, there are 1.3 billion people who already work remotely by some estimates, and, of the 157 million people in the US workforce, it's anybody's guess how many will insist on staying remote post-pandemic.

From a founder's point of view, once you can hire remotely, it doesn't matter if your best people are down the street, in the next city, state, or another country.

From a worker's point of view, if you have the talent and the skill, you can live anywhere and find work anywhere else.

The implications are staggering.

Radical Transparency: The philosophy that all information that *can* be made public *should* be made public within an organization. This allows any team member to have the same informational advantage as the CEO, for maximum empowerment in decision making.

HIRING REMOTE NUTS AND BOLTS

Obviously, there's no single path to hiring remote, but the following are a couple of indispensable advantages to deploying the Async Mindset when you get down to business.

Some of the radical differences with traditional hiring processes may surprise you.

- **Remote allows you to search for the *most precise fit* imaginable.** Looking for somebody who has had exactly thirteen months of experience in counting chickens and is also an expert juggler and a pescatarian? That person is likely out there, and remote allows you to find and bring that person onboard, and use him or her for exactly what you need. Be demanding. You don't have to settle for "close enough" anymore.
- **Gazing at the employee's curriculum vitae won't give you even half the story.** Google them, figure out what they're really about, identify proof of work. Engineers regularly send us their Git repositories instead of CVs—they know the proof is in the pudding. Good work leaves evidence, and that evidence is almost always easy to find. Also, instead of just observing, get in there and play with something that someone has built. Your experience will tell you more than any CV.
- **People are no longer looking for jobs, they're looking for projects.** Smart managers and workers alike know that projects can turn into jobs and even careers, but remote allows all involved to let the relationship grow at its own pace. Don't cling. Let the talent enter and exit your company as easily as possible. If you implement an Async Mindset, it doesn't matter whether they stick around for a day, week, month, year, or the rest of their careers, as long as they're bringing value.
- **Actively seek out self-starters who are ready to act independently without direction.** Employees who are dependent upon synchronous collaboration to complete their jobs generally won't survive in an async organization. It's a self-starter's game we play, and the industrially needy

are often weeded out quicker than they would be in an office.

With all of this in mind, just what makes remote workers good at their job? What are the Big Qualities you should be looking for?

- **Introversion:** Ironically, one of the clearest signals we've found when assessing new employees for long-term execution on deliverables is their modesty. Workers who need to be in contact with other people can still be critical team members in your company, but it's uncanny how swiftly they get replaced by more reserved team members. There are people who work blocks away from both of us, yet we rarely speak in-person. And there are people halfway around the world with whom we talk frequently. Obviously, it's not bad to be social, but those who don't need it are usually more successful than those who feed off it.
- **Independence:** If the core of the Async Mindset could be boiled down to a single tenet, it is this: Don't ask me what to do, tell me what you did. When processes and operations of the business are in place, there are really very few pertinent questions to ask. What's worse is that, even when they are well-meaning, synchronous interruptions reduce everyone's ability to execute on the deep work required to move the business forward. We're not saying that people shouldn't be talking to their coworkers, but 99 percent of what you bring should build culture and rapport in a genuine way. If you're asking questions that the platform already provides answers for,

you're generally ignored until you leave, or smacked with some very curt responses like "link attached." You simply can't respect other people's time enough.

- **Critical thinking:** The remote-first worker always knows how to manage fires in sequence. Should I answer three hundred similar customer emails or spend the next three hours fixing the source of their problem instead? The ability to be your own manager and direct your own decision making is critical to your overall success in an async environment. A lot of the time your direct report isn't even available and you can't wait around twiddling your thumbs—you need to make a judgment call. In those instances, the worst thing you could do is choose to do nothing at all.
- **Trust:** Needless to say, trust is a two-way street, but it can only be developed when you get past fear. That's why, in our company, we aim for radical transparency. Whatever we can share, we share—whether it makes us look good, bad, or ugly. How much money we make, what strategic decisions we've made, why we let a team member go, or even if we're going to make cuts inside the organization are all everybody's business, and that's how we want it. Why? Because we want all participants to think like an owner, so they can ask the kind of questions owners ask: *Where am I putting my time? Am I doing what I can for the good of coworkers? Do I have the ability to execute on a task or am I just faking it so I don't lose the job?* In a company where radical transparency exists on all sides, most large decisions are completely understood by all, because everyone has the same information.
- **A strong outside support system:** Do your workers have a good family life? Do they have strong social bonds

outside the workplace? It's important for people to have great relationships with their teammates, but in an async organization, socializing is a choice. A backdrop of strong bonds helps async workers get what they need socially "at home" more than on the job. A few years ago, we had a fantastic team member who came to us one day and told us he was accepting another offer for less money. Usually people leave for more money or at least more responsibility—leaving for less dough is a pretty big red flag. We talked with him and found out he had suffered a recent loss in his family around the same time he and his longtime partner had separated. He loved the culture of our company and the freedom it provided, but he feared that his loneliness would get the best of him if he stayed remote. We were proud of him for being candid, and grateful that he made a healthy choice.

- **Egolessness:** Of course, nobody can or should be wholly without ego, but the Async Mindset demands that you value yourself in the context of a community that you genuinely want to help. It's not about me and it's not about you, it's about us. We can think of no better example than one of our longest running team members, Justin. We hired him more than a decade ago for some paid advertising help, and he came back two weeks later stating that he didn't think he could deliver what we were asking for. He did, however, share that he had spotted about a half-dozen other problems with the business—*those* he could help with. Fast-forward a few years: Justin, of his own accord, led a complete rebuild of our technology stack to see if a version built from the ground up could replace our aging infrastructure. He committed nine solid months of his life to that project, and when it came time to discuss what version we should go with, he campaigned against his own version, admitting that the original was better.

People who can get over themselves are people you want in your async remote company. They make hard decisions, they don't hoard sacred knowledge, and they actively try to make themselves redundant to the organization, not because they're lazy or don't believe in themselves, but because it frees them to "up their game" and work on an even more interesting and complex problem.

HOW TO FIND REMOTE WORKERS—AND HELP THEM ONBOARD

1. **Build a pipeline.** Utilize job boards like FlexJobs, Remote OK, We Work Remotely, Remotive, and AngelList, as well as your internal customers and friends of employees.
2. **Implement an asynchronous job interview.** Always ask for a CV, but focus on the applicant's proof of work rather than explanations of previous roles. If he or she is an engineer, ask for a GitLab profile. If he or she is a designer, ask for the Dribbble account. If he or she is a marketer, ask to see the websites that person has worked on. Once you've got the proof in your hands, then you must insist that the applicant walk you through the processes used and what he or she did. Many people, when interviewed, will say they did X when the reality is that they were a very small part of X. Only someone

who was deep in the process will be able to describe how it was pulled off.

3. **Invite your second round to a video interview.** Always keep these video interviews brief. Y Combinator famously talks about how it can identify whether a start-up is one it can invest in *within five minutes.* We tend to spend about thirty minutes on a video interview, but if we're going to be completely honest, the last fifteen minutes are almost always a waste of time. You should already know if the person or organization you're interviewing can do the job before the interview starts; synchronous meetings are where you try to find out who they are. Bonus question: Ask yourself, "Would I voluntarily sit next to this person on an international economy flight?" If the answer is yes, they usually pass.
4. **Bring in a second interviewer to collaborate.** It's important that you don't discuss the candidates until you've both completed the process, so that you can separate signal from noise. If you both have exactly the same conclusions, great. If you don't, you may need another round of interviews. By operating asynchronously, you can add as many collaborators as possible, to help review the process and check to see if a given candidate is really the right fit.
5. **Whenever possible, hire on a trial basis.** It takes a few months before anyone can decide if a prospective applicant is a good fit, but the process is much more difficult in an on-premise company where you may bring somebody in for a month, then move him or her out a month later, disrupting

> the internal company culture. Hiring remote allows you to actually work with somebody right away, before you really start to *work* with them. A few months in, we like to have a "Speak now or forever hold your peace" meeting with managers, stakeholders, coworkers, and even subordinates to decide if someone's a good fit.

Remote Pioneers Sara Sutton and Job van der Voort: The Queen and the Prince

"We are naturally attracted to people who look or sound like us, or seem well-dressed or—whatever it is, we each have our own preferences. When you remove the visual . . . we're able to listen to their talents."

To really understand the remote difference in hiring and onboarding—not just how it works but what it can accomplish—you need to turn to Sara Sutton. Known in the industry as the "Queen of Remote Work," Sara is founder and CEO of FlexJobs, with more than twenty years in the online job market industry. FlexJobs is nothing less than the behemoth of remote hiring, providing a subscription-based service for employers in search of workers. Since the pandemic, it has become one of the biggest job sites of any kind, ever. In addition to her serious accomplishments in the trenches, Sara is a spokesperson for the ways that remote work can foster greater inclusivity, gender equality, cultural orientation, and "quirk tolerance."

We first met Sara between the chicken satay and the *nasi goreng* (Indonesian fried rice) in Bali at the first Running Remote conference in 2018. We'd invited her to speak and, in those days, we offered people a free flight, and by a free flight we're talking if there had been a ticket to sit on the wing we would have taken that one. Sara politely declined and flew thirty hours in business class at her own expense.

We were a little nervous about welcoming such a respected remote work pioneer to our conference. After all, we didn't really have that much experience dealing with pros at her level, and we knew she was basically doing us a favor. What could we really offer in return? To intensify matters, we didn't merely want her endorsement—we knew that a project like Running Remote couldn't survive without it.

Despite her royal standing, or maybe because of it, Sara turned out to be warm, disarming, and supportive in ways we never expected. Like so many other pioneers, she was a true proselytizer of the remote way, one of the first pioneers to be vocal with the general public about the Async Mindset.

More than five years ago, she was already talking about how she doesn't like video calls because they disrupt the workflow. "There are more efficient ways to communicate," she told us. We thought she was a bit crazy, then. But now we grasp that she was way ahead of the curve. She said that she found herself more comfortable and more attentive on voice calls, and to be sure, Sara is one of the most focused speakers and listeners we've ever come across.

She also sees a gender divide in the attitude toward video calls. "So many women I talk to share this sentiment, especially now," she says. "Prior to the pandemic, if you got on video, you did it professionally. You wanted to 'up-level' so that you were essentially talking to somebody as if you were in an office. You certainly wouldn't show up in a T-shirt with your dog in the background!"

Sara has witnessed the complete evolution of remote from a vantage closer than most. Her first company was located in

Connecticut, one of the first entry-level job sites in the space, started on a shoestring budget while she was still a student at UC Berkeley. At the time, back in 1995, job listings were still faxed and put into the big binders at career service offices. With fantastic foresight, Sara spotted a need.

"It was a mess," she says. "People would steal the binders. But also, if you were looking for an opportunity out of state, it was incredibly difficult, because employers weren't sending listings to some random university across the country."

That summer, Sara went back East and did an internship, often visiting with friends. When she told a friend's dad that she intended to study international relations, he said "You know, you don't need to get a *job.* You could be an entrepreneur." A light bulb went off. Based on her own challenge of finding work across the country, she dropped out of UC Berkeley to start the organization. At the time, campuses were just beginning to have email addresses and internet access, but still, the online employment concept just made sense. She got to work raising angel funds, hiring a team, and scoping the tech needs.

As the company grew, she wondered if she should return to school. "I pitched my team to work remotely for a year so that I could go back and finish my degree," she explains. "I was working East Coast hours and doing classes in the afternoons and evenings, then flying back to board meetings." The strategy worked, and by 2001 her outfit had been purchased by a public company—she was on her way to becoming the legend she is.

All along, Sara was keenly aware that the distributed model was growing in popularity with several of the companies she served. She often worked with people and teams that were several states away. She also saw how the basic values of good onboarding could play a part in remote hiring.

"I intentionally started FlexJobs as a remote company," she explains. "And I conscientiously thought about all the things I liked in an office, and all of the things I didn't. Of the things I liked—how could I translate them into a remote organization?"

Like many pioneers, Sara's attitude toward "the remote difference" went from intentional to very intentional along the way, customizing the remote experience for employers and potential employees alike. One of her greatest discoveries was the success rate for introverts working remotely. "I haven't done an internal poll, but I would guess at least 50 percent of our team are hardcore introverts. You realize that being in an office environment is draining for many people. It's exhausting to deal with office politics and interruptions. People like their space and their quiet."

In addition to what remote work could do for introverts, Sara also led the vanguard uncovering the way that remote work can foster inclusivity. She recognized that, by removing implicit bias, remote work opens the door for a fairer, more open-minded atmosphere. Among her inspirations, Sara cites a Harvard study that explored the predominance of men in the lead seats of city orchestras. Once auditions began to be held behind a screen, all that changed.

"We are naturally attracted to people who look or sound like us, or seem well-dressed or—whatever it is, we each have our own preferences. When you remove the visual, you realize what a great leveler it can be. People who are different or people with disabilities or people who are just not like us—we're able to listen to their talents."

At the heart of her contribution, Sara Sutton has been a warrior against the enormous resistance that remote work has faced, dissembling myths and assuaging employers' worst fears. "It always comes down to not trusting that your workers will do their job," she says. "That's the top level, and if you peel that away a bit, it means you don't trust your managers to manage well. Which really means that you don't trust the performance metrics that are in place and whatever structure you have around that. At the end of the day, these people are more comfortable doing helicopter managing, and it leads to this false positive."

The false positive is Sara's phrase for what we have referred to in this book as vanity metrics. "Somebody's in the office—they show up on time, they're well-dressed, you like them. And so, you give them the benefit of the doubt that they're productive and good for the team, good for the company. They might be good culturally. There might be some of that humor that does have tangential benefits and all of that." Her voice drops. "But that's really not looking at . . . are they actually good at what they do?"

She contends that the very act of implementing remote work creates a bellwether within organizations. If you have somebody who's not doing the job, you'll find out far sooner than you would have in a traditional office. That speed is doubled in the remote hiring process, where weak links can often be spotted before the person is even seriously considered. Discovery happens when employers get past the obvious—experience and skill set. "We ask questions in the interview process that try to pull out the moral character of the people we are interviewing," she says. FlexJobs asks for five words that friends would use to describe the applicant. "We're really attracted to people who say integrity. That's something you're not going to train for."

With great patience, she has played a dual role, educating both sides of the equation. In 2015, Sara did a survey in partnership with WorldatWork, interviewing three hundred large, North American organizations. The survey asked how many people offered flexible and remote work. About 80 percent of the orgs said they did. And of that 80 percent, the survey asked how many tracked the KPIs (key performance indicators) of their workers. A measly 3 percent said yes.

Once a new hire is onboard, she advises those employers who are new to remote to embrace what she calls "mistake over malice"—the fundamental belief that people are rarely intentionally negative. "At the core, what works for an organization is how do your employees feel the most valued and comfortable and productive."

Employers are often lagging way behind their hires when it comes to the Async Mindset. She notes visiting prime office real estate on Market Street in San Francisco, where half the staff were wearing headphones and nobody was talking to one another. "They're IM'ing each other, emailing each other. Zero contact." The scene highlights for Sara the costly misalignment organizations have with their office space.

Sara spots an even deeper irony with those Silicon Valley staples that have been hesitant and even sometimes overtly antagonistic to the development of remote work. "The Bay Area tech companies are the ones who have invented the very technologies we can use. The hypocrisy has been active, not passive, and some of the loudest voices saying they're going to ban remote work have unfortunately done it for optics. For example, they had negative quarters and internal management problems and they needed a win in the press."

The pandemic has forced the hand of many, but for Sara, the change still hasn't been deep enough. "You can't just institute remote work—you have to take a step back and look at the impact it will have on your culture. Otherwise, it's going to explode and then people are going to blame remote for that."

As for the future? "It's a pendulum. It's going to be messy, especially in the next five years. The nature of acquisition and retention is changing, but the driver is going to be talent."

"Our mission is to enable people in every country in the world to make more money for themselves."

If Sara Sutton is the Queen of Remote, and FlexJobs is *the* vehicle for online hiring, then Remote.com just might be the gas it runs on. Its founder, the affable Job van der Voort, is as close as remote gets to a living Prince of Remote. His company tackles the thicket of problems presented by global workforces, offering international payroll, benefits, and compliance services for distributed employees and contractors, taking care of everything from payroll and benefits to compliance and taxes, so that businesses can focus on people.

Speaking of people, Job is one of the rare ones who are just born to lead a billion-dollar company. In fact, if it were possible to buy stock in a person, we would recommend that you empty your bank accounts and invest in Job—he's that gregarious, that earnest, that smart. For a long time, he was the man behind the curtain at GitLab, helping that company grow from five people to the multibillion-dollar behemoth it is today. Job always recognized, however, that he wanted to do his own thing. He found that commitment in 2019.

"July of that year," he told us, "my wife, Carla, was hospitalized. She was pregnant with our daughter, but began an early labor at thirty-two weeks. A week later, June was born. Healthy, but she would have to stay another three weeks in the hospital before she could come home with us."

The first day in the hospital, Job wrote a Slack message to his colleagues, saying he couldn't worry about work for at least another two months. He was concerned, but his newborn came first.

Then came the surprise.

"When I came back to work two months later, there were no frantic demands for my time. In fact, there was nothing but support and people telling me to take it easy. I was able to be a father first and a worker second because of async."

Job got to thinking: *Why can't everyone on the planet enjoy a professional life that didn't disrupt personal life—a life that allowed people to focus on . . . life!*

A Dutchman with a background in neuroscience, Job cut his teeth on models of modern machine learning, recording data from the brains of rats to analyze nuances about how the brain encodes information. At the heart of this study is the concept of signal detection—discovering a discrete signal within noise. It had long-reaching implications on the way Job thinks.

"How do you reach a particular skill in a company, or a skill in a product? You're going to have errors, you're going to have problems, but how do you uncover the signal you're looking for?"

One way to think about signal detection relates directly to the async remote model. "To detect signal," Job says, "you have to constrain the modes of communication as much as you can." With this in mind, Job made a jarring discovery: Organizations have a tendency to burden themselves with "cycle time" waste.

"Most companies radiate information through synchronous work," he explains, "which is just the most stupid thing you could do, because it's a waste of time, and it's ephemeral. You speak it out and it's gone."

Despite his love of science, Job knew he didn't want to be a career academic, reporting to bosses and angling for funding. When he met his wife in Portugal, he took a crack at a start-up, but quickly ran out of money and ended up at GitLab, a fully distributed company. He worked from the Netherlands for cofounders in Ukraine and coworkers in Serbia. As an international worker, he began to grasp the complexities of global hiring and contracting. In time, Remote.com was born. They've raised $196 million in 2.5 years, and Job van der Voort is the spearhead of a true tech unicorn that is breaking open the world of employment.

"If you're a US company," he says, "and you want to hire someone in another country—well, you can't just do that. You can't just give them a US contract. It's meaningless to them, and they can't do anything with it."

That's where Remote.com comes in. It arranges and manages contracts, payroll, benefits, taxes, and more, making sure each employer and employee are locally compliant and in the clear for all pertinent labor laws. They're in fifty countries at the time of writing this book, but they plan on being in eighty countries next year.

The basic premise of the company has far-reaching implications for the globe. "Our mission is to enable people in every country in the world to make more money for themselves." Every arrangement is unique. In some countries, Remote .com opens a little office—one even has a single chair and desk, just to say it exists there. Some countries don't need healthcare benefits, because healthcare is free. Some countries pay for pensions or stipends, others are relatively undeveloped tech-wise. In Kyrgyzstan—a landlocked country in

Central Asia where only half the population even has access to the internet—Remote.com tracked down and hired an amazing engineer.

"It's a bureaucratic nightmare," Job says with his infectious laugh. "The amount of stuff I have to print, sign in different ways, in different formats, with different stamps, and proof of identification."

The pandemic meant near-absurd hyper-growth for Remote .com as it went from 30 to 330 employees. Despite the chaos, the influx of massive funding, the acquisition of new contracts, Job faces it all with stalwart positivity.

"I think the biggest change that we see today is that individuals realize that their work, which happens behind a computer—there's no reason for it to only happen in the office anymore. And, so, it doesn't matter as much as what a particular employer wants, because that individual knows he or she can just get up and move to another employer that allows them to work remotely. They can live wherever they want."

Imagine a world where work and where you live are totally disconnected, worldwide.

"Just one example—take the average salary in India," Job says. "It's something like $10,000 for civil engineers, for the more in-demand roles. Now, if you're in India and you enter the global market, you have the opportunity to increase your salary by something like 8,000 percent. It's unparalleled, and it will change everything, everywhere."

Employee Net Promoter Score: One of the most important measures used in asynchronous teams to measure employee satisfaction. The main question usually asked of employees is, "On a scale of zero to ten, how likely are you to recommend working for (company X) to others?" You calculate total ENPS by subtracting your detractors (those who choose zero to six) from your promoters (those who choose nine to ten). Passive responses (seven to eight) are not calculated in the score. Final scores can be anywhere from minus-100 to 100-plus. Most remote async organizations have ENPS scores above fifty. Below thirty is generally considered a poor place to work.

REMOTE CULTURE 101—FOR POTENTIAL EMPLOYEES AND EMPLOYERS

Async culture is a reality—but the most misguided thing you can do when considering a new position is look for the kind of culture you find in so-called regular offices. It's not there.

To understand and spot async culture, you have to readjust your lens on the word *culture* itself.

Most industries define culture in terms of how employees socialize together when they aren't working. In remote teams, it goes the other way around: Culture is how you work together—and socializing is the byproduct. Doist[5] recently captured the essence of this in a brilliant, simple pie chart (see figure 4).

To put it another way, culture isn't something that you create from work, it's something the work itself creates. That's why one department may behave very differently from another culturally, even if they're both hitting their metrics and getting the job done. One team sends goofy internet memes on Slack, another's out there doing VR game sessions, a third is yapping about politics on Zoom calls. It's "culture" because it's their way, and to meet a team culturally, you have to meet them where they are.

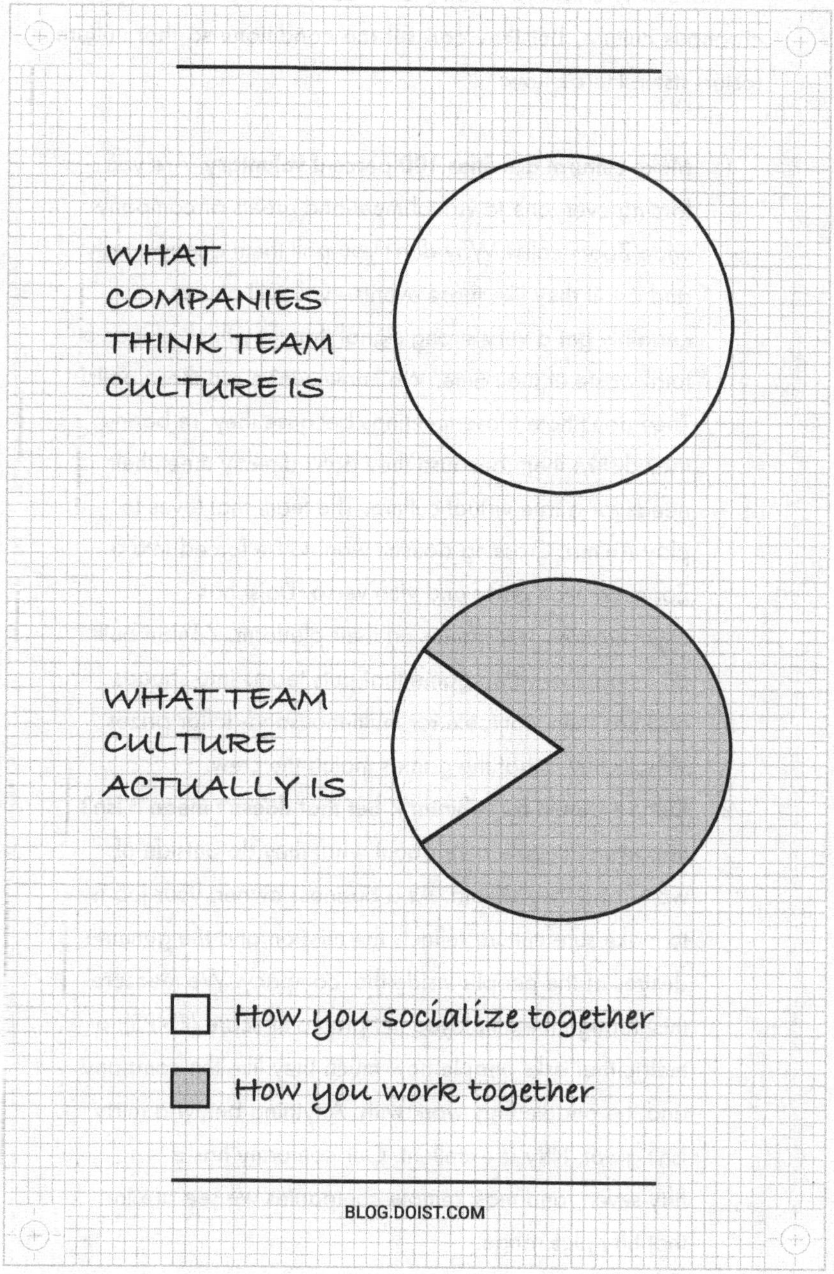
WHAT COMPANIES THINK TEAM CULTURE IS
WHAT TEAM CULTURE ACTUALLY IS
How you socialize together
How you work together
BLOG.DOIST.COM

FIGURE 4

That's why employers can't technically "create" remote asynchronous culture, but they can set the conditions so that culture fosters itself. Here's how:

1. **Make cultural activities 100 percent voluntary.** Are you forcing everyone to virtual meet-and-greets or company-wide Zoom calls? Why don't you poll them anonymously and ask if they like those events—you will almost certainly get a very strong signal that they think of it as a total waste of their time. We know, we've run those polls! They don't hate those meetings because they 're boring; they dislike them because they don't directly meet their needs for a true virtual culture. The team that loves to play Animal Crossing doesn't want to be forced into a Zoom cocktail party and vice versa. Doist has asynchronous text games on their platform. X-Team built an interactive video game that puts teams into squads and has them compete for multi-thousand-dollar prizes. What's key is that the games match the crew.
2. **Culture should be voluntary, but that doesn't mean it isn't important.** People care about what they do outside of work, and they should. As a business owner, your job is to make sure culture reflects the mission and the genuine desires of the people inside that company. We measure this through the employee net promoter score (ENPS), a metric that asks people how much they like the company and the people they work with. Anything below a thirty isn't great. Fifty is excellent. Our company has a fifty-seven, and most remote companies we see are in that fifty-plus range.
3. **One of the greatest culture assets in a remote async company is, ironically, the lack of synchronous**

interruption. Coming together with team members is important, but it has its place and time. Most remote pioneers we've studied say they prefer intensive rather than extended meetings. When you go synchronous, go as high fidelity as possible. How can you turn an audio call into a video call? How can you turn a video call into an in-person meeting? Generally the higher you go on the async fidelity scale, the shorter the meeting has to be. This provides employees the added benefit of less distractions, so they can spend more time with family and friends and disconnect from their work world. Deeper contentment leads to deeper commitment. It's a strong cycle.

4. **Spend time thinking about how you can WOW your company.** Create experiences for them that are extraordinary. We usually take our entire team out to yearly retreats in an exotic location where we reforge our culture and build spirit toward our next year. If you can't do something in-person due to logistics or costs, feed your internal culture through events. A great example is X-Team—it makes in-person events truly epic. You can catch a glimpse here: https://www.youtube.com/watch?v=EdWlF3z0JQo.

In async, the development of a working culture is not just a by-product you hope for. It's a priority you actively cultivate. Define a budget for it and make it count.

When we do get together, we make it as useful as possible.

First and foremost, we tackle problems we can't solve or issues we can't resolve asynchronously. It's a process of weeding out. First we tackle any technical obstructions to achieving goals. Often, along the way, we discover the problem is not technical at all—a team member may have a problem with another employee, or may have a problem in the home. Or may even have a problem philosophically about the project. Whatever the issue is, the key is to uncover it and face it without fear.

One thing we don't do: We don't look at the numbers. Everybody's already seen those.

We celebrate our successes instead of focusing on our failures. We all know where we're not doing well. Privately, these issues can be addressed. Publicly, we compliment and praise as honestly and enthusiastically as we can. Even though you should be egoless in async processes, the fact is that it's human nature to love to be complimented in public.

The in-person team retreat is pretty much a staple of remote companies—most do them at least once a year. We usually boil it down to three locations and have the company vote on where to go. The gathering provides everyone in the company an intense period to work on the business without any of the distractions you'd get in your usual workweek or personal life. It's also a time for us to pause and think about what's next.

Often on these retreats, we marvel at the degree to which a company culture has created itself.

Michael Koenig, Remote Pioneer: Double Agent at Large

"Trust is earned in drops and lost in buckets."

Nobody knows the psychological nuances of hiring remote and people management in a remote setting like Time Doctor's COO, Michael Koenig of Ann Arbor, Michigan. He's both expert and voice of reason, having been present for the ascent of Automattic, one of seventeen pre-COVID-19 companies that had a remote headcount of more than a thousand before 2020. Creators of WordPress, Automattic is something of a zenith—the very pinnacle of what pure remote can be. Still, for an early newcomer, it was daunting.

"They were communicating in a bug ticketing system at the time, along with a slew of IRC (internet relay chat) channels and internal blogs," he explains. "And it was all very natural for them. I'm a pretty extroverted person . . . and here I was coming into a close-knit community who were all pros at this type of work. It was jarring going from a colocated space to suddenly not being around anyone—not hearing voices, not seeing faces."

Trained in person-to-person business, he occasionally perceived a terseness in the communications from engineers he had to work with, and he was thrown. In one instance, an engineer wrote *Why did you do that?* Michael explained and the engineer quickly responded by writing *Well don't do that.*

"It was hard not to feel put down."

Luckily, a colleague explained that this was just par for the course—everyday async engineer talk, and a reinforcement of one of the remote-first golden rules: Always assume positive intent.

In time, Michael befriended the engineer and they really bonded, but more important, he came to understand that a certain kind of async message didn't amount to terseness at all. "There was no malicious intent. It was just . . . a very different personality type at work, all about brevity. For me, that was a huge adjustment."

Remote software engineers, he explains, tend to build their relationships through the creation of code and the problems they solve together. For those who aren't in the thick of it, it's not uncommon to get cold feet when it's time to post a question to a public IRC or Slack channel. "You're at a company like Automattic. They built WordPress, one of the most consequential pieces of software on the internet. These folks are brilliant. I'm not going to lie. I felt a little insecure."

To cope, Michael would end up pinging people on the side for advice privately, before he had the confidence to start operating in the public chat channels again. Slowly but surely, he began to help others adjust to the same communication challenge. He encouraged newcomers to get past vulnerability and ask what they needed to ask. "The goal was to get confident enough so that you could hop into that main chat channel and ask anything. It's essential that people remind themselves that everyone here trusts them and their expertise . . . that everyone wants to see them succeed."

At Automattic, it was traditional for every team member to have the word *engineer* in their title. At a company retreat, CEO and founder Matt Mullenweg asked Michael what his role was. Michael said, "Well, frankly, I'm in business development so I schmooze a lot right now."

He was soon given the title "schmooze engineer."

Michael had acquired what you might call "double agency"—as a people person who grasps, at a very granular level, the powers and deficiencies of remote communication. It made him acutely aware of the difficulties posed for proper hiring and onboarding remotely. As Michael explains it, an async company like Automattic was "hierarchically flat" in the early days, because it started that way, growing as an extension of the collaborative way open source software like WordPress was created. What this means is that every new team member that comes along must learn to share not just in the process and the information, but in a kind of transparent group consciousness—the whole operation as an open dialogue built on always assuming positive intent.

On the bright side, this means that all workers are empowered to act as intentionally and deliberately as never before. On the challenging side, Michael points out that remoteness can lead to a kind of transference where you can feel isolated from your team, even when you interface with them every day. Michael calls this phenomenon "absence paranoia"—negative thoughts as a symptom of working away from your colleagues. He says that managers and team leaders have to actively combat this unspoken dread by grooming people to always assume positive intent and report problems before they fester. "Culture comes from the top," he says, "so, if you want people who are joyful, you have to help them find joy beyond the project at hand, and you have to do it at the outset."

Michael posits that, when people don't know you in person, they can only infer your personality from the characters you type and what you write. "Things go off the rails when you try to be too cute or say something that can get misconstrued."

For Michael, it all comes down to perception. "In a remote async environment, perception truly becomes reality. When you feel wronged, when things get heated and you're about to respond to an email. . . . Well, in this instance, being remote and operating async are an asset. You are able to draft a response, sit on it and keep it in your drafts, go for a walk, sleep on it, and then revisit your draft with fresh eyes. That's when async becomes beneficial."

For the new hire, Michael notes that "one bad judgment or interpretation can really live on. Trust is earned in drops and lost in buckets."

Moreover, for employers doing the hiring, and for new hires coming onboard, a higher level of sensitivity is required in remote work. "You have to consider not just the personality differences, from one American to another, from engineer to businessperson, you also need greater cultural sensitivity that comes in order to work effectively with someone in India or Thailand or Africa. There are *big* cultural differences—the American experience is very different from what the rest of the world experiences. You need to be more mindful of what you say and how it's perceived than you would in a colocated work environment."

Michael adds that the ultimate hiring goal of a remote organization is not to "convert" onboarders to the corporate doctrine, but to help everyone be and reveal their truest selves, using their quirks and cultural differences for the company's good. "After all," he says, "we're hiring you because of what *you* bring as an individual that uniquely contributes to the cultural fabric of the company."

OUR WEIRD QUIRKS DOC

The key to understanding onboarding is that it's very much like any other relationship, a two-way street. Let's get to know each other, openly and honestly. Let's share the good, the bad, and the ugly, and find out what we all need. This is more difficult in an asynchronous remote team, since the fact is that you don't pick up as many of the subtleties of a person online.

We like to put our cards on the table, to a fault. That's why we've created formalized "quirks documents" to hand out to newbies (see figure 5). These documents are developed through a simple but hilariously entertaining exercise: Get three of your closest friends and ask them what they'd tell another friend of theirs if they were about to start working for you. You need friends who will be real with you. How real? Very. They need to be able to say

BLUEPRINT TO LIAM AND HIS QUIRKS

Quirk: Noun (plural quirks), an idiosyncrasy; a slight glitch, mannerism; something unusual about the manner or style of something or someone

1

I'M AN ENTP

ENTPs are inspired innovators, motivated to find new solutions to intellectually challenging problems. ENTPs enjoy playing with ideas and especially like to banter with others. Google ENTP personality types to learn more about me.

2

DECIDE

Decisions over options is always my preferred way of working. If you have to bring me options, tell me which option you're leaning towards. If you aren't leaning towards an option, then you haven't thought about it long enough.

3

SPEED OVER PRECISION

We are a startup, move fast and break things. If you aren't making mistakes from moving quickly then you aren't moving quickly enough. Asynchronous communication requires us to be faster than a brick and mortar company.

4

NEED TO KNOW BASIS

If you need to help make a decision ask yourself: Does this help achieve my task or goal? Does this slow down Liam? Is this a blocker issue? Is Liam blocking me or not? The more information you leave out, the faster I can make a decision.

5

CLOSEST TO PROBLEM

Whoever is closest to the problem is the person I will trust to make the best decision. Usually I can't make as good of a decision as the person who has been dealing with the problem on the front line.

6

I GO ON TANGENTs

I like to talk a lot (see ENTP) and this may bring us off topic. You need to refocus me and make sure I stay focused on what I need to give you to succeed. Basically, tell me what to do and if I'm blocking you, tell me quickly either in person or in email.

7

QUANT ALWAYS WINS

I won't be able to support you in a decision if you don't have quantitative data to back it up. Bring data to back up your decision and always ask yourself if you took the opposite view, would you make the same decision?

8

MY GOAL IS YOU

My goal is to make you as successful as you possibly can be. I will invest time, money in feeding your passion. If you don't like your job don't be afraid to tell me. Moving you to something else is better than you providing bad results.

I value decision making above all else. I'd rather you make the wrong decision than none at all.

QUIRKS BLUEPRINT	
TITLE	Staff.com/TimeDoctor
CREATOR	Liam Martin
VERSION	1.0 - 10/5/2016

FIGURE 5

out loud some of the things you may not even want to admit to yourself.

The quirks might embarrass you at first, but ultimately, they'll give you a better chance of survival if you share them.

21 TOP ETIQUETTE RULES FOR WORKING IN AN ASYNCHRONOUS REMOTE COMPANY

1. Don't ask a question without looking for the answer in the company's internal processes document for at least five minutes. (If that document takes you more than five minutes to digest, it needs to be improved.) Process documents are not there to give you fish; they are instructions on how to fish for yourself.
2. Don't ask people what to do, tell them what you did. Almost any decision can be reversed within twenty-four hours.
3. The person who is closest to the problem is usually the one who should make the decision about that problem.
4. Create a sacred work space that is separate from all other spaces in your life. It doesn't matter where, but if you reserve and protect that space, and make it just for work and work only, your productivity will skyrocket.
5. Identify your weaknesses and share them with everyone—your manager and coworkers and everyone else. They'll appreciate your candor, and it will ultimately make everyone more productive.

6. If you can, do epic stuff while you work—travel the world, take on big projects, embrace your passions. People rise to their level of daring.
7. Don't bring toxicity into your home life from work and vice versa. If you have a problem at home or work, deal with it there, and your family and coworkers will thank you by following your example.
8. Set work hours for yourself and stick to them. Nobody likes an email at 2:00 a.m., and if you send those expecting a quick response, you're a bad coworker.
9. In case emergencies arise, set up ways to get in touch with team members 24/7, but only trigger that process if it's actually an emergency. Don't be the boy who cried wolf.
10. Don't check your phone during video calls. Everyone sees your eyes looking at your phone, but they won't call you on it. *We're* calling you on it. Stop.
11. We don't care how you deliver work, but if you do it better than anyone else on the team, it's your obligation to show the team members how they can do it better.
12. Have a dead man's switch on decisions. For example, *If you don't respond to an issue in forty-eight hours I will choose option B.* That way, nobody can block you from moving a project forward.
13. Related: It's a sin to *not* make a decision and move a project forward because you're scared that you'll make the wrong choice. Make your moves, and any self-respecting manager will give you his or her support.

14. Have a good webcam that doesn't make you look like a potato. Have a good microphone, too.
15. Remote workers should be responsive and reliable, but not necessarily accessible. If you send people messages and expect immediate responses when it's not an emergency, you are disrespecting their time.
16. Spend that extra minute or two rereading emails and instant messages. Can you simplify? Can you fix the wording to make the message easier to understand? Your coworkers will thank you and follow your example.
17. Always assume positive intent with every message you receive. Textual information can be interpreted differently by different people. Assume it's positive unless you *directly* know otherwise.
18. You will probably be working with multiple cultures. Obviously, you should not assume yours is superior. Also, if you're concerned about something cultural, ask your manager or the coworker directly in a respectful and egoless manner.
19. Be honest about your passions and you will usually receive more of that type of work.
20. Use a schedule and share it with others in your company so they know when not to interrupt you.
21. Respect the time of others as if it was your own. Time is tricky. You can't keep it, you have to spend it, and once it's gone, you can never get it back.

CHAPTER 6 TAKEAWAYS

1. Remote companies usually involve multiple nationalities, currencies, time zones, and cultures. The old-school human resources models don't apply.
2. Hiring remote always means looking for the very closest custom-fit, no matter how specific. With an international array of options, count on finding the right person.
3. Use the applicants' tools, read their code, and give your experience more weight than their CV history or what school they attended. The proof is in the pudding.
4. Look for self-starters who exhibit qualities like introversion, critical thinking, trustworthiness, a strong outside support system, and egolessness.
5. Build a pipeline through remote jobseeker services such as FlexJobs, and, wherever possible, hire on a trial basis.
6. To find the right person, work past your implicit biases and focus on talent.
7. Watch out for "false positives" or vanity metrics, such as looks, charisma, and even promptness, working long hours, and affability. Just because someone seems like a good worker doesn't mean he or she is actually good for the company.
8. When considering developing an async culture for your new hires, keep in mind that activities should always be voluntary and custom-designed to teams

and their genuine interests. Wow your employees with a great experience they won't forget.

9. Retreats for remote-first companies are their own breed. You don't need to focus on data, since it's already been shared. Instead, celebrate successes and create bonding experiences.
10. Hiring and onboarding also means acclimating new employees to the existing environment. They need to both understand the existing languages and feel free to present questions.
11. A higher level of sensitivity is required in the remote workplace, since people from different continents and utterly different walks of life are called upon to cooperate with one another.
12. The remote workplace has its own brand of etiquette, but most of it boils down to this: Be responsive and reliable, and respect the time of others as if it were your own.

SEVEN

The Perils of Going Remote . . . for Companies in Transition

At the Running Remote conference, where hundreds of businesses approach us to learn the very best methodologies for functioning remotely, we often find that we need to give transitioning companies—those that have previously existed for some time in a colocation office—a simple but stern warning:

> If you've never worked like this before, going our way will be scary for you. You aren't just going remote, you're reconfiguring the heart of the way your business operates, and at first, you probably won't agree with a lot of what we're saying. Some of our attendees tell us that every bone in their bodies is telling them that this is not the right move. But you're going to have to take a leap of faith here because there probably isn't any other way to build a successful remote company. Take our word for it, we've checked.

> Our promise: Allow your organization and yourself to evolve to an Async Mindset, and you will see creativity, productivity, and profits grow faster than you ever imagined possible.

Not all those companies are ready to take that leap of faith. We can't tell you how many people first attend our conference or have us consult for them, and then don't take any of our suggestions. Sure enough, they come back a year later saying they're stuck with the same issues they had in the first place.

Often, the problem is that companies in transition have already begun to focus on the wrong elements by the time they get to us. Their line of inquiry tends to reflect a basic misunderstanding about the nature of remote work and, by extension, asynchronous work:

- What kind of tools are best for remote?
- How do you deal with conflict in a remote meeting?
- How do you make major business decisions without being near one another?
- How do you make sure your employees stay engaged?
- How do you build company culture in a remote team? We used to have pizza Thursdays—do you deliver the pizzas to everybody's house now? Or should we maybe have virtual-reality parties instead?

The uncomfortable fact is that these are the wrong questions to ask. Even if we could answer them, we wouldn't be able to take these people where they need to go. As so many of the remote pioneers agree, these companies have put the cart before the horse.

A deep Async Mindset and methodology are the first things to work on. The pizza parties will take care of themselves.

That's why we're going to show you some of the companies that have dared to embrace asynchronicity to greater and greater degrees—to help you build confidence in the idea itself.

In fact, it's a pleasure to have so many great examples to share. Everything we always hoped would happen to remote work has happened—we just had no idea it would all happen so fast.

If you told us in February 2020 that 80 percent of all knowledge workers would be working remotely within thirty days, we'd call you a nut job. And yet, the world didn't just embrace remote work, it *converted* to remote at warp speed. Ironically, our own Running Remote conference, booked for April 2020, had to be canceled, to our deep chagrin. We lost hundreds of thousands of dollars by canceling. Even worse, we knew that people out there desperately *needed* the secret sauce we had to offer like never before.

In January 2020, our average customers were fast-moving agencies and start-ups that had an eye on the officeless future. Fifty days later, we were suddenly dealing with Fortune 500 powerhouses and actual governments. All these giant entities shared some serious anxiety about going remote, so much so that we started calling them Pandemic Panickers—a term we use to this day.

There were no ten-thousand-employee remote companies before the pandemic. Not even one. Today, our friend and colleague Ryan Chartrand, who runs X-Team—a cooperative of location-independent developers doing project work for

Fox, Dell, Intel, and Sony, to name a few—recently told us: "I'm getting a dozen emails a day from friends and clients asking, '*How the hell can I build out my multinational ten-thousand-plus seat organization remotely?*' I'm totally out of my depth here. How am I supposed to help a company like that?!"

"We're getting messages like that, too," we said. "It feels a little like, tag—you're it!" Though we're running companies of hundreds, not thousands, we realized that if we don't help them, nobody will. We're the only ones equipped to help these organizations out of panic and into remote.

To be blunt, this influx of strong interest from traditional outfits has been a paradox from our point of view. On the one hand, the world was suffering from the spread of a deadly disease. On the other hand, we were witnessing our greatest dream realized—the adoption of remote/async work on a grand scale by people who said they *never* would even consider it. To complicate matters, many companies taking the leap were doing it wrong, and flailing and drowning. We, the remote pioneers, were the only ones with the lifejackets—and everyone else was sinking fast.

Even many companies with the best intentions were imploding, because they didn't understand that remote work is not about software tricks—it's about a complete restructuring built on the twin firmaments of autonomy and deep work. Without the guts or the means to do that radical reimagining, many giants quickly went from success to Zoom fatigue without understanding why they were suffering.

As remote pioneers, witnessing the worldwide transition has sometimes been comical, sometimes heartbreaking, sometimes frustrating. To see so many companies fumble, dither, mishandle, and act in haste on such a widespread scale has been hair-raising to say the least, but as the world gains its sea legs, we're confident that the basic tenets of the Async Mindset will come to the fore.

> **There were three giant mistakes many made right out of the gate, all of them interconnected.**
>
> **The first was not understanding how differently you must communicate in a remote organization.**
>
> **The second was continuing to manage by presence.**
>
> **The third was failing to recognize that the old-school manager has no place in a proper remote-first organization.**

We knew you'd all come along eventually. Welcome.

Every company has to live through its own rebirth, and rebirths are painful.

In January 2021, *Forbes* provided a comprehensive list of big companies taking the leap, and the variety of trials and tribulations hint at the chaos underfoot.

- Question-and-answer website Quora announced in June 2021 that it had adopted a remote-first model, noting that 60 percent of its employees had chosen to work from home beyond the pandemic. They plan to convert their offices in Mountain View, California, into coworking spaces. The CEO himself said he would not visit more than once a month. (His only requirement, however, shows the degree to which some leaders are still clinging to the old modes: He has stated that employees must turn their cameras on for all virtual meetings.)

- One month after Quora made the move, pharmaceutical company Novartis announced a shift from manager-approved remote work to manager-*informed* remote work, meaning employees can choose to work how, when, and where they want. Novartis also said it would expand its mental health benefits as part of this initiative.
- Nationwide Insurance made one of the swiftest transitions to remote work at the height of the first-wave coronavirus crisis, with more than 98 percent of its twenty-seven thousand employees working from home. The experiment worked so well that Nationwide has recently announced plans to downsize offices—from twenty to just four.
- Credit-card start-up Brex informed its leadership team that they will telecommute most days, but offices in major cities will remain open. "Off-sites will be a big part of Brex as a remote-first company. As soon as COVID-19 is over, we'll have frequent company and team events (for example, approximately once every two months) focused on building deeper team relationships, rather than heads-down work," cofounders Henrique Dubugras and Pedro Franceschi wrote. Brex, which adjusts employees' salaries based on geographic markets, also announced that those who relocate to areas where pay rates are different may see their compensation change. However, they promised to hold off on those adjustments until September 2024.
- The mighty cloud-storage company Dropbox announced in October 2020 that it would become "virtual-first" going forward, with collaborative spaces called Dropbox Studios where they used to have offices, starting in San Francisco, Seattle, Austin, and Dublin. They also are promising "nonlinear workdays."

- Music-streaming company Spotify has announced a "Work from Anywhere" policy in February 2021, offering employees a choice of working fully from home, from the office, or a combination of the two. Spotify also pledged to give workers more flexibility on which locations they chose to work in. If employees choose to work from locations that aren't near a Spotify office, the company said it would offer them a coworking space membership if they want to work from an office.
- After surveying employees, Salesforce learned that 80 percent of its workers want to maintain a connection to a physical office space. In February 2021, the software company announced it would permanently switch to three ways of working: fully remote, office-based, or flex. The majority of Salesforce employees will work on this flex policy, meaning they will work in the office one to three days a week for team collaboration, customer meetings, and presentations.
- But perhaps the most startling is REI, the outdoor retailer familiar to any American who loves camping. It just announced the sale of its brand new, unused eight-acre corporate campus in Bellevue, Washington. CEO Eric Artz said the company will "lean into remote working as an engrained, supported, and normalized model" for employees.[1]

Everywhere you look, the lines on the map are changing. Some of the most interesting cases are those with the greatest resistance.

Next, we'll look at just such a case.

Vidyard Makes the Move

> "Our office, the light fixtures, the graffiti on the walls, the cool aspects of the environment we created were not our culture."

We get it: Not all offices are created equal. For some companies, physical space is mere commercial real estate, rentable and interchangeable. For our longtime friends and colleagues at Vidyard, the office meant home and their "happy place."

An online B2B (business to business) video messaging and video hosting company, Vidyard was entirely office bound before the pandemic, working out of three stories in a building in the city of Kitchener, Ontario (pop. 242,000). Suddenly forced to go remote, they started the quarantine with serious misgivings about what they thought would be the impending loss of "social capital."

Although Vidyard was a tech company whose systems were not so very hard to replicate remotely, cofounder and CEO Michael Litt was particularly thrown—he had personally designed their office space and had a great love of wandering the halls, sharing ideas verbally, picking up on company culture. He was devastated to be leaving his baby, his headquarters, behind. In fact, Litt had been one of the few guys we knew pre-pandemic who insisted that remote would *not* work for a hyper-growth company.

Some founders act out of fear. That's not Michael Litt. A self-described adrenaline junkie and "learned extrovert," he's also a driver of British-made race cars and has been in more than one serious crash at 135 mph. Still, nothing could have prepared him for the pandemic crash.

"Physical space is just so important to me," he confessed to us. "[Our old office] embodied the sense of culture, of how you bring yourself to work. And for the longest time, I confused the concept of an experience that a space can create with the culture of an organization. The gatherings, the parties, I conflated a lot of those experiences with our culture. But our office, the light fixtures, the graffiti on the walls, the cool aspects of the environment we created were *not* our culture—they were just a single part of a much broader ecosystem."

Litt wasn't converted overnight. As the pandemic forced Vidyard's hands, there was nothing for it to do but act fast, shutting down large portions of the office and keeping a few discrete areas open as "hotel desks" that they could keep clean enough while practicing maximum social distance. Over the course of the pandemic year, more and more of these mini-sections went dark—the great shutting off.

As Vice President of Marketing and Chief Video Strategist Tyler Lessard remembers it: "Our building was three floors worth of space. If we could've just maintained a single floor or something like that we would have . . . because of the investment we made. But it wasn't an option."

The company went fully distributed. Much to their chagrin, the doors were locked and Litt went into a kind of panic. "What is this gonna mean for our business? What is this gonna mean for our economy? Is this thing gonna take the knees out of our customers?" Like a survivalist preparing for catastrophe, he fully expected to shrink the company by three-quarters.

Something funny happened along the way, however. After a few months of begrudgingly adapting to remote life, Litt and Lessard could not deny one hard fact: The numbers not only did not substantiate their fears, company productivity went up more than 10 percent, and several major process renovations were getting implemented, improving work life all around. "We started to look at the success of our new methods and say, 'Well, if we go back . . . this stays. And so does this. And this.'"

In fact, Vidyard leaders frequently found themselves asking, "Why didn't we do it this way five years ago?"

By April, demand was through the roof and Vidyard's whole MO (method of operation) had to spin 180 degrees. They went from 170 to 260 to 350 employees in the blink of an eye. Hyper-growth not in spite of a closed office, but because of one.

Vidyard turned to executive coach Hubert Saint-Onge for guidance. They went from asking "How will we survive?" to "How can we best manage this rapid expansion?"

"We're blessed to be in a market that's growing all the time," Lessard observes, "but it just started moving faster than ever. We built to ensure we could quickly scale. The team was ready, and our systems were best in class. At the same time, all of a sudden our costs were lower than ever."

To their credit, Vidyard quickly figured out that it couldn't ride through this with a mere cosmetic change. "There was a period of ambiguity where there were more questions than answers," Lessard says, "and we were trying different things, sorting things out. We hit a point where we started to understand what was working, what was resonating with people."

After the initial shock, Vidyard got intentional about how to work in a distributed environment. Suddenly there was no advantage to either being in the office or on the Zoom call. Processes that had operated intuitively but did not materially exist began to create problems, so solutions were written down, a process we detailed in chapter 4. Best of all, Vidyard knew it would have a challenge onboarding new people, so it wisely jumped to develop a whole new hands-on approach to coaching individuals, using its own digital tools to advantage. What Lessard describes as "tribal knowledge" began to be deliberately shared with newcomers.

Crucial to its evolution, the pandemic forced Vidyard to hire outside its small town, which led to the sudden acquisition of some powerful name talent, including a public relations leader from the far-off land of San Francisco. "In the old world, I would have tried to prioritize a local hire," Lessard says. "In *this* world, I don't have the same concerns like, 'Oh, she's not gonna be as well-integrated with the team because she's not here.'"

In addition, longtime employees were now commute-free, more rested, and easily more dedicated. Several reported that enhanced connections with family helped with overall well-being, which led to a surprise bump in productivity.

Here's another counterintuitive aspect of Vidyard's successful transition: By collaborating less, employees found themselves to be less annoyed, with greater time and space to get the actual work done. The enforced privacy directly connected to a sense of autonomy that drove the company forward.

Also surprising—whatever office politics remained quickly improved in tenor.

Before the pandemic, Litt and Lessard had made a habit of identifying what they call "f**kbergs"—minor toxic incidents (or people!) in the office that were likely to combine and create much larger problems down the line. (The term is actually now part of their process documentation.) What was shocking, however, is that going remote radically reduced the number of these sightings. Litt and Lessard concluded that social distancing not only helps slow the spread of coronavirus, it also helps slow the spread of negative employee behavior.

As we said, we've witnessed dozens of examples of companies that fumbled in the transition to remote. Vidyard is just one example of well-handled metamorphosis. They made it work because they knew they couldn't simply transition—they needed to be reborn.

Perhaps the most dramatic of changes is that Vidyard was allowed to view its own products and services in a new light. Because it is a digital company, Vidyard was literally forced into the "life position" of their average customers, and this new point of view produced invention and reinvention.

Vidyard makes an asynchronous video product with vast benefits for internal communications. In fact, its product faces down one of the great problems of remote work life: Zoom fatigue. Vidyard formats can be no longer than ten minutes and speed controls enable the viewer to watch at 2x, so that every player can absorb all content and expected outcomes before having to waste a single minute on Zoom.

"You know how it is," Litt says. "When you have a meeting, the most senior person, the most extroverted person, the most opinionated person often takes up 90 percent of the conversation. And you don't get to hear anything from other people in the meeting, right? Introverts, people who are deep, deep thinkers and contemplators, keep their mouths shut."

Through async video communication, the playing field is leveled. "Individuals who might not, you know, want to speak out for obvious reasons . . . now they have a place in a space to contribute. We're going to actually get a much more diverse spectrum of opinions that allow us to enrich our experience and make our company more productive. No more stuffing people in boardrooms."

The most charismatic person isn't always the one with the best ideas. This process of weeding out is one of the greatest superpowers of asynchronous teams, which always measure based on merit, not mystique.

The educational video formats Vidyard provides have quickly been adopted by educators, sales leaders, and communicators of every age and stripe as they simultaneously helped the company survive its very own rebirth.

Today, Litt is optimistic about the move, and excited about the future. He's okay with radically downsizing the company's physical space, even as it is growing exponentially. Vidyard is planning on designing a new collaboration center that will be quick and easy for local employees, kind of like an internal coworking space where people can come to work (or not), depending on what they actually need.

"My new idea," says Litt, "is we're not going to have ten floors in one city. We're going to have one floor in ten cities, spaces where people can drop in, get that connectivity going."

Litt's ultimate discovery is the key realization most companies in transition usually miss at first and come to eventually rely on, and it's one of the cornerstones of this book:

> **"We finally realized that the only way we could help our people be productive," he reports, "was to leverage asynchronous technologies. You can't expect people to jump on Zoom all day long, that's just not realistic."**

He smiles and adds, "The concept of the office, the cool chairs, you know, the fun space . . . all that needs to go into the rearview mirror."

RULE #1: DON'T LOOK BACK

What Vidyard beautifully sidestepped is the first mistake most companies make: trying to recreate the office. The really scary thing is that this Band-Aid may even work for some organizations for months or even years, but eventually the rhythm implodes, with bad operations and overly complex processes infecting one another as company culture deteriorates.

The other great blur that Vidyard managed to see through is the common misconception that transitioning to a remote/async model is just kinda sorta a nice or convenient thing to do. They knew that the new situation demanded a bigger change, and they acted accordingly.

> **Believe us when we say that your competitors are already pivoting to async, full stop.**

And, without a doubt, they are going to produce more efficient companies that grow at lightning speeds. If you don't get a handle on how it's done, you're probably going to get blown right out of the twenty-first-century marketplace.

From the helicopter view, here are the broad elements you'll need to master for a sound, remote-work transition:

1. You'll need to build an asynchronous communication model *before* you get started or, at the very least, plan for one while you're transitioning. How can you annoy your team less so they can do more? It's a question you should be asking yourself ten times a day.

2. You'll need to poll and align your entire team, front-loading them for working in an asynchronous model. There are people who initially see async as boring, and you will need to work with them to show them the real value of the process. Get everyone on the boat and make sure you're all rowing in the right direction.
3. You'll need to build and digitize all your company's processes, as we've touched on in chapter 3—an arduous beginning that will end up being a compelling function for hyper-growth. This may seem incredibly tedious at the onset, but trust us, this is the only way you can achieve scalability whether you're in an office or not.
4. You'll need to develop a reporting structure that allows all workers to report their core numbers to everyone in the organization. Ideally (and this is a tough one for some) every single employee should have as much information as the CEO. At its core, this means **you should empower your employees with all the data at their fingertips so they can all think like an owner**.
5. You'll need to heavily reduce or cancel all meetings about metrics. Meetings are for discussion about issues that come out of the numbers, they are not a place to discuss the numbers. Time is money—stop wasting it.
6. Last but not least, you'll need to measure the rate at which your employees embrace all the adjustments that async work entails, and provide course corrections as quickly as possible. No backtracking allowed.

Once underway, you'll have to ask yourself to take a cold, hard look at the changes. How do you know your remote team transition is going well? What should you look for? Here are the *first* questions to ask:

- What's your employee attrition rate? It had better be lower than when you were in the office, and if it isn't, you need to find out why.
- What's your employee net promoter score (ENPS)? If you didn't measure it before you went remote, take a look at its current variance—is it going up or down?
- **Are you meeting virtually more or less than you used to meet in person in the office? If your in-person OR Zoom meetings haven't decreased at least 60 percent, you aren't really async yet, and therefore, you have yet to master remote-first work.**
- How often are you having collaborative disagreements—more or less than when you were in the office? Do they resolve?
- Who hates remote work right now in your company? Do they feel safe enough to be honest about it? For the record, the haters usually boil down to a few core "types," Often they're super-extroverted and love the "audience" of an office, and/or they have no social life and work is their outlet, and/or they have kids and those kids have boundary issues, and/or they're a micromanager and need to monitor everyone's every move at all times.
- Are employees engaging in virtual social communication where nothing is forced?

- Are you discovering processes that need to be built that you could never have detected inside of the office?
- Are you building these processes for the long term with open access?

As Tomas Pueyo brilliantly observed in an *Uncharted Territories* article called "Remote Work Is Inexorable," not everyone is embracing the move to remote at the same rate, but it's especially the *incumbents*, successful old-school behemoths, who most want to protect the status quo. No surprise then to hear an old-schooler like Goldman Sachs's CEO David Solomon making the cringeworthy remark that "[Remote work] is an aberration that we are going to correct as soon as possible."

Even though we know beyond a shadow of a doubt that these naysayers are on the wrong side of history, we don't judge them too harshly, because we understand the underlying fear and tension. Going remote without guidance is a challenge, especially for the entrenched. The fact that no two transitions ever unfold in quite the same manner adds to the confusion.

We remember talking to a billion-dollar company about going remote, and they just kept getting stuck on their ten-year corporate leases that would cost hundreds of millions of dollars to break. They said, "We just don't know if we can survive without going back to the office."

"Here's the bad news," we said. "We're pretty sure you *won't* survive if you go back."

- **Hybrid Organization:** A company that has a blend of both remote workers and on-premise workers.

Cutting-Edge Clorox

Of all the companies to grasp the power of async, you'd think that one of the least likely would be The Clorox Company, the American manufacturer of cleaning products and other household essentials that got its start as the Electro-Alkaline Company in 1913—the year the parachute was invented. After all, isn't Clorox the very definition of traditional? They make a product so common and ubiquitous that the very name has become synonymous with general cleaning powder, much in the same way everyone incorrectly calls all disposable handkerchiefs Kleenex.

Sacha Connor began working for the Oakland-based $6 billion company in brand marketing at the dawn of the millennium. She spent fourteen years there, leading product lines from Pine Sol to Brita to Hidden Valley Ranch. In 2010, after commuting for six years, Sacha had her first child. One year into motherhood, she asked Clorox if she could keep her job but move back to her hometown of Philadelphia. They said "Okay, but . . . let's see how it goes."

The three-month experiment turned into an eight-year run, with Connor running remote and hybrid teams, helping them to learn how to work across distance. She found that the lessons she was learning and perfecting were applicable—surprise, surprise—across the organization.

Today, Connor is founder and head of Virtual Work Insider, a company dedicated to training teams, executives, and companies in the skills to work in a hybrid and remote environment, but her expertise didn't happen overnight.

"Working fully remotely is hard, but hybrid is even harder," she explains, "because of distance bias." Distance bias, a term created by the NeuroLeadership Institute, is our brain's natural tendency to put preference on those people and places that are nearer to us. Connor felt it daily at Clorox, and it was a constant challenge to mitigate and overcome.

There is also, she says, something called "recency bias," whereby we tend to put more importance on the people and things we've seen or heard from most recently. "If you've got a team of five people, and two of those people are really good at reaching out and staying top-of-mind . . . the next time you as a manager need to assign some work, your natural tendency is going to be to think of those last two people you talked to."

Connor suggests posting pictures of your entire team near your computer, so that you can keep the whole group in mind.

The "headquarters"—even for a rock-solid entity like Clorox—is giving way to the distributed model. When Connor broke from the fold, her bold act of independence highlighted the biases at work at headquarters, and things began to change.

When the pandemic hit, Clorox was more prepared than most. With 8,800 employees around the world and a tech center in Pleasanton, California, the company was hit with a conundrum. Because it made products that disinfect, its goods were more in demand than ever. Of course, manufacturers still had to be on-site to make the products. Furthermore, some R&D employees still had to go to the lab to work on product formulation.

But for everyone else? 100 percent remote.

The learning curve was intense for many, but they instinctively saw that making it work would put them ahead of the pack. The mission was for employees to thrive wherever they lived. Anyone who worked with a screen was given the mandate to learn to lead from a virtual place.

As Kyra Zeroll—Clorox's director of marketing and another remote pioneer—points out, the challenge was as emotional as it was technical. "We were able to give tips and tricks about how you keep social engagement," she recalls. "For those who are not used to working remotely, you get exhausted. You don't realize that you might be sitting all day long. How do you build in those breaks?"

Going forward, Zeroll believes that things will likely progress on a case-by-case basis. "What lessons have we learned from this and how do we take that into the future? I absolutely bet that we will be more hybrid than we were in the past."

THE SEVEN DEADLY SINS OF REMOTE TEAM TRANSITIONS

1. **Recreating the office.** Remote isn't just recreating the office remotely, it's a different animal altogether.
2. **Meetings as "show 'n' tells."** When it comes to taking up someone else's time, less is better. Focus on what others can do to actually help you, instead of dwelling on what they can already find out asynchronously.
3. **Not talking about the issues.** Get behind the metrics, explore their deep hidden meaning, and be open to every opinion offered.
4. **Punching the clock.** Does the length of time matter if your people get the work done on time? Measure for productivity and engagement, not how much time they spend on the computer. Repeat after us: Thou shalt not manage by attendance.

5. **Not providing advanced materials.** If we don't already know everything you want to talk about, you're wasting everyone's time.
6. **Narrowly defining company culture.** What really binds the company together? Hint: It's bigger than remembering to give Karen a cupcake on her birthday.
7. **Drowning in work for its own sake.** Repeat after us: Thou shalt get a life (and let your employees have theirs).

CHAPTER 7 TAKEAWAYS

1. Transitioning to the remote/Async Mindset requires courage, patience, and the willingness to embrace counterintuitive thinking.
2. Basic questions like which tools to use aren't enough. You need to be ready for a whole new methodology that reimagines your organization from the top down and the ground up.
3. This methodology is built on the foundation of autonomy and deep work.
4. In a remote organization, you communicate differently.
5. In a remote organization, you don't manage by presence.
6. In a remote organization, there is no place for old-school hierarchies.
7. Transitioning to remote without guidance can be disastrous. Many major companies fumble their way through with great loss.

8. On the other hand, those organizations that have approached the transition with forethought and bravery often discover growth in surprising ways.
9. Broadly, the transitioning company needs to start with an async communication model already in place; they need to be ready for team resistance; they need to fully digitize all processes; and they need to "open the book" so that every employee can get to all information.
10. In the remote-first, async organization, every member is called on to think like an owner, and value one another's time.
11. The only meetings an async company needs to have are those gatherings where issues are discussed. Meetings about metrics or "show 'n' tells" that could be presented asynchronously are a waste of time.
12. The transition to remote is itself a measurable process. Only a cold, hard look at the numbers will reveal whether you're doing it right.

EIGHT

The Async Leader's Guide to Unmanagement

It should be clear by now that what constitutes strong, everyday leadership in a colocated company just won't work in an async remote environment. In particular, the old-school manager barking commands and demands, telling everyone how to do their job, is anathema in a functional remote culture.

> **In fact, if there is one management principle the remote pioneers all agree on, it is this: The remote team leader must be absolutely "agnostic" toward everything but results.**

It's not as easy as it sounds, and the act of letting go requires some counterintuitive thinking.

For instance, a lot of the remote pioneers hire workers who appear to be "lazy people," because they are often the kind of people who have developed the strong habit of getting things done in the most efficient way possible. It's a remote-first paradox. These people might look like they don't do much, but they are often the team members who figure out how to build themselves out of the process.

There is, however, one major caveat: You have to give them complete freedom to discover it and trust that they are brave enough to make themselves redundant. Amazing as it sounds, they know it's seen as an asset rather than a liability.

As early as 2013, a BBC article[1] was already noting that some savvy software developers were known to outsource their work to others. One US employee spent his work days surfing the web, watching cat videos on YouTube, and browsing Reddit and eBay, as he paid a fifth of his six-figure salary to a company based in Shenyang—they did his job for him. Was he breaking the rules? Sure, and many employers would feel cheated, but we think this guy should have been given a medal. Or, better yet, an employer adopting the Async Mindset would ask him how to scale this and make everyone more efficient.

Learning how to relinquish control and create the space for every player to "self-commit" is challenging, but when you enter the async zone, there is simply no substitute. Without that self-commitment, you will never get an employee's best. That's why our bottom-line management policy is "Don't ask me what to do, tell me what you did." It's a discrete form of unmanagement.

Of course, we aim to help those employees who really and truly need our help, but we absolutely hate trying to teach people who are closer to a problem than we are. If too much help is required, it usually ends with them getting fired. The harsh reality is, in remote-first companies, we can very quickly find somebody better within minutes. In an on-premise model, replacing that person could take months.

"Going agnostic" and embracing a full async environment requires a level of honesty with yourself and faith in your charges that the old-school manager could not likely comprehend. In order to grant every team member true dominion over their responsibilities, you've got to genuinely believe they can take the wheel.

Which brings us to another "A" word that is the cornerstone of async unmanagement: autonomy.

THE TWIN REVOLUTIONS

When it comes to embracing complete and utter autonomy for every employee in the workplace, the remote pioneers were first-to-market. But the truth is, it was an idea whose time had come. It had been incubating for more than thirty years, long before there was even a public internet to speak of. As early as 1975, Edward Deci and Richard Ryan first developed their revolutionary concept of self-determination, positing that the ability to act autonomously could lead a person to greater fulfillment in life. Notably, they argued that this autonomy, the basic human need for feeling choiceful, had the power to radically fuel work performance, often in counterintuitive ways.

Meanwhile, as these brilliant psychology professors developed their ideas in the abstract, a second revolution was underway, the technological advances that set the stage for remote pioneering.

For many decades, it seemed that these two revolutions were at odds, at least on the surface. After all, wouldn't a digital world mostly undermine human autonomy? Couldn't computer micromanagement, automation, and relentless measurement trap every venture, every employee? Simply put, wouldn't more tech turn us into the slaves of robots?

Actually, the twin revolutions were secretly linked in positive ways that could not yet be appreciated. Nobody could see that it was possible to cultivate a technology-driven work environment that matched the spirit of autonomy.

Whether or not the remote pioneers stumbled onto this confluence is up for debate, but the fact is that they were the people who embraced maximum autonomy just as soon as the technology allowed for it. Having met some of the most colorful pioneers in this very book, you can probably surmise that it's a personality type: These people don't just "like autonomy"—they're allergic to being held captive in any way, shape, or form.

What that means is that the remote pioneers, for the most part, are not natural managers in the old sense—many of them probably are not that comfortable telling others what to do. The platform is the middle man, reversing the equation, whereby direct reports are telling managers what they need.

We've had many difficult meetings where direct reports have come to us saying, "It's quite clear that the current process isn't working, and I have three different suggestions on how to move this number, but don't know which one to choose." Shared radical transparency provides clarity of success or failure, and the person closest to the work usually becomes aware of that success or failure first.

The platform, not the manager, dictates what to do next.

What this unlocks is an acceleration that very few "tethered" companies have experienced, but it's becoming more common. What the pioneers have unleashed just happens to be a gift for everyone.

As Andreas Klinger, whom we met in chapter 5, puts it, "At the end of the day, the best practices in remote are really just best practices of management in general. Wherever asynchronicity drives efficiency, growth, and accountable employees, the issue of office or no office is irrelevant."

> **"Managers," he explains, "have always been communication hubs. They communicate decisions from above and problems from below. If you've got a process in place that can do the communicating, it saves a lot of effort."**

Once processes can operationalize buy-in and delineate expectations, all one-on-one time can be reserved for what Andreas calls "context"—people stuff, family, daily life rather than the work itself. Context, he insists, is no small thing. "A good person in a bad context won't perform great."

THE ASYNCHRONOUS AUTONOMOUS ORGANIZATION: A CLOSER LOOK

It might sound like a paradox, but an autonomous organization is a collection of independent actors. Some may be employees, others may be contractors, some will hail from consultants' agencies, others from software platforms and AIs, and more. What matters most, however, is that all are given the highest level of independence as well as the power to make real decisions in the organization.

As we've illustrated, the autonomous organization is intertwined through communication, process, and measurement. Regardless of role, every party is connected to the whole. By being radically transparent and measuring everything inside the organization, and then, by extension, giving back those measures to everyone, every party is empowered to make independent decisions that move the operation forward. No need for gatekeepers, micromanagers, middle men. All are united in their independence.

> **In an async autonomous organization, platforms are the office.**

- Platforms give everyone an informational advantage, allowing them to think and act like owners of the company.
- Platforms allow you to start anywhere in the process. Since there are no gatekeepers saying, "Work on A, then B," you can begin where you'll be most productive. Focus on what you're good at and build from there.
- In an open platform, everyone can also see what you're doing in real time. Once you get past the newness of this experience, you reap its enormous benefits: The ability for all to help, course correct, encourage, and supplement.
- The informational advantage of platforms cuts both ways: Everyone can see everything, but everyone can also not pay attention or not pay very close attention to anything in the business that they are able to ignore without affecting their role. As CEO or head of HR or director of marketing, what information is important for me to know *today*? If it isn't useful to focus on R&D right now, I can ignore it.

- As Ryan Chartrand of X-Team explains, platforms make the value you add to the organization measurable like never before. It soon becomes crystal clear whether you're a boon or a drag on the organization.
- It's also important to note that your value becomes obvious to everyone—not just to your manager or your boss—since everyone can see what you're up to. By the same token, you (and everyone else) can measure your manager's or boss's value in exactly the same way.
- The platform fosters democracy, by providing dozens if not hundreds of virtual project rooms, whether it's a Zoom room, a Slack channel, a Trello board, or a Google Doc. Anyone in the company can jump into that room, read all the information, and add his or her two cents without being disruptive in any way. That is the beauty of async.
- The platform leaves a reliable history. Everything is recorded, measured, analyzed by the platform, and it can be pulled up and reanalyzed whenever necessary.
- As a business owner, you can be in ten meeting rooms at once in a platform-based workspace—something never before possible in a physical office.
- Again, from Chartrand: If a department head wants to know if a particular developer support person is doing well, he or she can easily go look at the statistics in the company's email platform and track all manner of pertinent data: How quickly that support person responds, what the response rate is, how many emails have been sent out this week, how many emails were received, how many cases actually

closed, and more. No need for lie detector tests—the metrics tell all.

- Platforms broaden knowledge for the curious, allowing every team member to learn all parts of the process. You might work in sales, but now you can see exactly how the hot dogs are made, how they are packaged, how they are shipped, how they are marketed. Moreover, you may even have a few ideas about how to do all those things better—your feedback is encouraged.

> **Platform-augmented Management:** The concept that organizational responsibilities such as project updates, metrics-setting, and course correction can be delegated to the platform itself, freeing up leaders for "contextual management"—people stuff, family, daily life, inspiration, and encouragement, rather than the work itself.

Ryan Chartrand, Remote Pioneer: Chartrand's Army

"The scary thing for a lot of people is that it means that your performance is actually finally based on output. The value you add becomes apparent because the platform makes it obvious."

Just what does management mean when your teams are async, super-skilled, highly mobile, and spread over the globe in every time zone?

Ask Ryan Chartrand. He's more than just a pioneer—he's pushing remote to the next level, creating a whole new language for async management. His company, X-Team is the ultimate expression of *distributed*, with more than seven hundred developers who travel the world, living and working as digital nomads while working on the very hardest problems in tech today. Sony, Fox, Twitter, and Dell are just a few of its clients.

But its advances are about more than just travel, more than just location.

What really sets X-Team apart is its complete and intentional embrace of autonomy and *unmanagement.*

Do you want to work today? What do you want to work on? How do you want to approach the work? These are the questions Ryan's team can ask themselves every single morning.

No wonder then that he attracts the top .1 percent of engineers—the cutting edge that insist on freedom. It's an elite squad, and they wear the X-Team brand proudly. Not everybody makes the cut.

Incredibly, Ryan cut his teeth at age twelve, managing online gaming communities. He learned how to build teams and how to build culture remotely and internationally. His tools at the time were MSN Messenger, AOL Messenger, and IRC. Still, despite dealing with the savviest engineers and the most powerful corporations in the world, the underlying principle of his leadership style has not changed.

"Autonomy," Ryan explains, "really comes down to that 'proactiveness muscle.' Do you have the ability to move forward on your own?"

He notes that not all cultures have the same relationship with autonomy, which makes managing internationally all that much more complicated. For example, workers from India tend to be permission-based—so are workers from old-school corporate America. They need the boss to sign off on every major move.

"The most common thing that you'll see," he says, "is the twiddling thumbs, the person who has no problem charging you eight hours for the day for doing absolutely nothing, because you didn't give them a task that day. It's just that sense of, 'I don't want to get fired. So, I'd rather do nothing than potentially get myself fired by doing something that I wasn't supposed to.'"

Ryan believes that it can take years to break someone out of that mold, but if you dig hard enough, you'll find people in every country who have already broken the mold themselves. "Maybe it's just in their DNA, I'm not sure."

Sometimes, even the mostly autonomous employee will balk if the situation is critical enough. If there's a major bug in production on a Friday night, and the DevOps manager who usually must approve all releases is out of office, will their next-in-line have the courage to push through the hotfix? For Ryan, it's more than just an abstract scenario—X-Team is juggling international contracts with international workers round-the-clock, and there's no magic formula for making sure the work gets done. "There's a misconception that remote companies have all these secret tools that allow for a continuous work cycle," Ryan says, "but at the end of the day, we use the same platforms everyone uses—Google, Slack, Trello, and so forth. The future of work is platform-based."

Ryan recalls his first job, working at the top newspaper in San Diego. "They had the most exotic office—right out of *Mad Men.* You'd walk through the big pearly gates into the pretty lobby, people bustling, walking around. And I thought, *This is what a company is; this is what a business is.*"

Today, however, five to ten platforms allow every company, including that newspaper, to accomplish more efficiently everything the office did—in record time, and better, and more integrated.

"There's no waiting for the conference room to get opened up," he says. "There's no waiting for your boss to allow you to come talk to them in their office. You just start *doing* and everything is constantly moving forward."

Ryan has a special distaste for those platforms, like Gather.Town, that try to recreate the office in virtual space, undercutting the value of real platforms. "If I want to know if your support person is doing well, I can look at the statistics that tell me literally—how quickly he responds, what the response rate is, how many emails have been sent out, how many we've received, how many were closed.

"The scary thing for a lot of people is that it means your performance is actually finally based on output. The value you add becomes apparent because the platform makes it obvious."

For the aces at X-Team, however, it's downright startling how so many independent, forward-moving, totally autonomous top-rankers are able to collaborate as much as they do. "You'd expect them to stay in their silos!" Ryan says.

Instead, they're given one managerial mandate: *demo often.* In programming, it's de rigueur to see the demos as quickly as possible, for instant adjustment and correction. X-Team extends this to the entire organization—they want to see immediate demos from finance, marketing, anyone at the company. "We want to know," Ryan says. "Give us that midway progress so we can make sure something wasn't misunderstood or there isn't something that needs to pivot . . . or maybe we just need to pull the project at this point because it's not living up to what it should be. In the platform-first world, it's easy to test."

To allow the blackbelt employee to thrive—especially when you're operating in multiple time zones—an enormous level of trust is required for the async manager. "You are really forced to let go of that top-down control," Ryan says. "But from a psychological standpoint, giving a highly talented, highly independent person autonomy unlocks in him or her a commitment to the company that just doesn't exist in a lot of companies. It only works with certain types of people. You're going to unlock a selflessness that comes with knowing that, 'Okay, great, this company respects me—they've given me this freedom—and I'm going to return that.'"

THE ASYNCHRONOUS AUTONOMOUS ORGANIZATION: CHALLENGES AND SOLUTIONS

Without a doubt, there are hurdles, pitfalls, and obstacles that are totally unique to an asynchronous/autonomous environment.

For one, the async model makes it excruciatingly clear who isn't performing well on a project and who needs to be reined in. The metrics tell all.

That's why the Async Mindset manager focuses on EQ (emotional quotient). There's no need to harp on the numbers—the platform has already spelled them out, exposing weak points without mercy. For the employee with a fragile ego, this level of exposure can sometimes be detrimental, and it's on the manager to keep the employee fighting for progress and improvement.

Brittle employees aren't the only casualty where metrics are concerned. Sometimes, an excess of data can lead to a dangerous management stasis that must be overcome. Making the wrong decision is often better than making no decision at all.

As Ryan Chartrand puts it, "I'd much rather you do something that's moving the company, even if it takes us a step back. . . . The number of things that move forward always outweighs the number of things that pull you back."

To this end, when faced with a disagreement in an autonomous workforce, management often ends up solving it by choosing *both* paths at the same time if possible. If the cost is low enough to deploy a thirty-day experiment, try both options and revisit the disagreement in a week, a month, or a year. One of the most glorious benefits of remote work is that experiment costs are exponentially lower than they would be in an in-person company. Need to decide to go with Asana or Trello for project management? Deploy both for a few months and see what happens. Yes, it's messier, but nobody in an on-premise team would ever suggest building two offices to see what happens.

As we've tried to make crystal clear, old-school hierarchies dissolve in a remote-first, async context. Sometimes, that freedom brings a few bad apples—it's inevitable. The platform's ability to measure the organization should control for these anomalies, but they do slip through the cracks. With this in mind, management must calculate their operational speed. Do you want to move slower with fewer bad apples? It's a tough decision. We tend to prefer fast, because experience has shown us that quick and cheap imperfect action leans into success, but if you're performing brain surgery or running a nuclear reactor site, you can't afford bad apples, and total autonomy is probably not for you.

To that end, there *are* cultures that just don't work autonomously, we admit it. As Ryan Chartrand points out, companies that don't have to deal with different locations and different time zones will not *instinctively* embrace total autonomy with the speed that a remote-first company simply must. Autonomy spurs innovation, which drives some organizations, and is a detriment to others.

Autonomous work is fantastic for highly talented, highly independent people. The state of autonomy unlocks in them a deep commitment that is hard to replicate by any other means. Still, big freedom can bring "altitude sickness" to those who are used to an infantilizing permission-first work culture. If all your life, your job never required you to solve a single complex problem on your own, the freedom can be disorienting.

If you're afraid to speak up, if you're afraid to take the lead, if your fear of being fired outweighs your respect for the truth, autonomy is going to feel like an uphill climb, and the async manager needs to help facilitate the journey and minimize discomfort.

Obviously, the async manager needs to start with empathy, especially for those who seem to need their hand held. There comes a time, however, when every async autonomous team member must let go of your hand. The wise manager knows they won't succeed any other way.

HERE'S WHAT A TRULY AUTONOMOUS ASYNC EMPLOYEE LOOKS LIKE

Our former director of recruitment, Loreen, was a perfect example of the spirit of autonomy. She always told us what she did, and never asked what to do.

Loreen lived the majority of her life in Cebu in the Philippines. In her younger years, she had lost her husband. Bringing up two children there is very hard for single parents. Still, she was determined to survive. By the time she got to us, she was a self-guided missile—you could show her any target and she'd figure out a way to get there, dead-center.

Even when she knew very little about how to build or support a sales force, Loreen took the task on, and within a week she had built a full-fledged international team with strong built-in processes. A month later, we asked if she could head up our retreat, and within weeks, she'd assembled a crew and flew the whole gang in from dozens of countries.

Loreen didn't just make things happen. She often told us what we needed before we knew it.

Her motto: "I'll find a way."

LEADERSHIP THE ASYNC WAY

In an async company, you lead more than manage.

Leading constitutes creating a vision for where the company wants to go, inspiring people to get to that vision every way they can.

Where management's primary job used to be measuring inputs and forming the day-to-day targets, those tasks have been utterly usurped—and improved on!—by metrics and process. The one thing the machines can't do is get people excited about the future.

Difficult manager-employee conversations do take place, but they have a different tenor in the async environment. If you have to let somebody go, for instance, it's usually the leader's fault, often boiling down to the wrong hire or an insurmountable goal, poor resources, weak data, or just not knowing enough before trying to hit an unruly target.

The accent on metrics also helps async management resist the urge to pick favorites, since quantitative results are already public knowledge.

What's important is that the async manager encourages his or her team to never fear showing their work, even in its infancy. Early feedback means early course correction.

The async manager understands that being radically candid starts at home. You show your team *everything*, including how much money you make, how much profit is at stake, the strategic direction of the company, and every one of your primary concerns. You aren't just being candid for its own sake. By aligning all employees to the mission—and all its accompanying challenges—they are going to receive that information as a gift. And if the information scares them and hastens their departure? That's good, too.

In our own organization, we show everyone every single thing, save for internal HR issues or anything that might constitute disrespect to an individual team member.

The idea is to clear a path for imperfect action, executed as quickly and as cheaply as possible. Encourage people to make mistakes and tell you about them in detail. The only sin is stasis.

In an in-person environment, this proclivity for mistake-making and mistake-sharing would probably bruise a lot of egos, but in async management, we turn our lens on the metric, not the person that delivered it. In fact, we always encourage the team members to feel free to suggest giving the job to someone else if they don't think they're a match.

By the same token, team managers in an async environment need to see themselves as caretakers rather than representatives of their teams. The team "belongs" to the company, if it belongs to any entity at all.

What all this lack of hierarchy finally amounts to is that the leader him- or herself should be the most redundant piece in the async organization. They can participate in innovation, they can help move the business forward, but they should not, cannot, must not hold sacred knowledge.

If the leader can't go on maternity leave without negatively impacting the business, you have not maximized your processes, and it's back to the drawing board.

HOW DOES THE ASYNC MANAGER MEASURE HIM- OR HERSELF?

What are some good KPIs for the async leader? To know, you need to ask yourself the following questions.

- What is the ENPS (employee net promoter score) score of your team members?
- How much time are they spending on meetings? We think a good target is between 10 and 20 percent of their work week.
- Are targets being reached? Usually, if 75 percent of targets are being hit, you're in a good mix, but higher than that and the targets need to be harder. Lower than that and you're failing—you need to figure out why.

- What're your anonymous ENPS numbers? This survey asks a simple question: How likely are people to recommend working at your company?
- What is your team doing with their time? Poll them. Ask them what they want more or less of. It's critical toward identifying whether you're moving in the right direction. If more than 10 percent of your average workweek is synchronous, you're not where you should be.
- Distribute anonymous surveys on leader performance. Philip Rosedale, founder of *Second Life*, the first metaverse environment, famously polled his staff yearly, asking if he should be replaced. If more than 50 percent of responses said yes, he promised to leave. Anonymity gives you the real story. Always focus on egolessly moving the company forward versus wasting your time and theirs with worthless pandering.
- Study employee turnover. It's simple to measure—12 percent is the average, and 9 percent is the average for remote teams according to an Owl Labs survey. If you're remote, that's your target.
- How long does it take to close tasks? They should be completed within a 20 percent variance of the time allotted, whether you're behind or ahead of schedule. Analyzing why you have or haven't completed in time is critical to moving the team forward. Was the task too easy? Did you have all the information available to you? Did the team members require more training to get it done? Were they the right people for the job?

Strive for the same level of honesty you hope for in every one of your team members. It's not about you, it's about the organization.

A WHALE OF A PROBLEM

Before closing out this chapter on the power of async management, it is our responsibility to address what happens when you *do* go sync. Much as we try to minimize it, it happens. Here are some ground rules.

When you have to go synchronous, make it as efficient as possible. Stay focused on the issue. You'll be surprised to discover how often the real issue is *below, beside, or behind* the issue you're discussing.

For instance, maybe you're not hitting a target because someone's family member is about to undergo surgery and energies are distracted. Fair enough. Once you get that data on the table, your job as a leader is to clear the block as gently and pragmatically as possible.

A few years ago, some members of our team were hit by a Category 4 hurricane. We remember getting a Slack update from one team member showing us that all he had left to his name was his MacBook. His family's home had been completely destroyed.

How do you "manage" a situation like that? All we could do was reduce his anxiety as much as possible by getting him and his family set up in a hotel and a coworking space until he could rebuild his home.

You can't stop hurricanes, but you can lead the way to safety.

During the first month of the pandemic, another team member sent us the scariest Slack message we've ever received: *There's a body in my front lobby and I don't know what to do.*

We immediately got our employee on a Zoom call. He couldn't stop hyperventilating—he could barely get a word out. Still, what we did understand was that, as he had stepped out of the elevator on the ground floor of his condo in the morning, there was a body bag being taken away by police in hazmat suits. One officer told him he needed to return to his apartment ASAP—there had been a serious COVID-19 outbreak in the building.

Understandably, our employee was worried about what he had touched. He didn't have any masks, and he didn't have enough food to make it through the week. We sent groceries, disinfected them, and did what we could to let him know we were with him.

In an async environment, the manager is a facilitator and a helper, not a watchdog.

Sometimes, we go sync and everything seems to fall apart. In fact, one of our biggest sync failures happened in the middle of the pandemic. We lost the vision for which customers we were after as a company, and realigning that target demanded a real-time session.

In every business, you need to figure out what kind of customer you're hunting, be they Mice, Rabbits, Deer, Elephants, or Whales.

A company like Facebook, for example, mainly goes after Mice—small, individual users who give over their information in exchange for being ad targets.

A remote-friendly company like Shopify goes after Rabbits—small businesses that need a quick and easy way to make an e-commerce website.

We had historically been Deer hunters, going after small to small/medium businesses that have ten to five hundred employees. During the pandemic, however, we were inundated with requests of a larger scale. Suddenly, the whole world needed a time analytics tool for remote teams. In fact, we were even approached by a G20 *nation* who wanted to know how it could deploy their 400,000-plus employees remotely.

This sudden success began to distort our thinking, as sudden success often will. We started daydreaming—*Hey, maybe we're not Deer hunters after all.* Maybe we're actually a Whale-hunting operation. Like Captain Ahab, we went half-nuts with the prospect of the Big Kill. We started aiming our sights on 10,000-plus seat organizations, plotting to move our product "up the market—where the real money is."

The reality is this—going upmarket might be the right move to make, but there are right and wrong ways to make the move. You can almost never "skip animals." To get to Whales, you need to become a seasoned Elephant hunter.

This discovery was a rare insight that could only have come to us synchronously.

"So how many of these Whales have we actually *gotten* this last year?" we asked the team of vice presidents who had assembled to discuss planning for the next year.

"Honestly?" one responded. "I think we had two in 2021 and fifteen in 2020."

We'd already seen the metrics. "Okay, so then what's the plan to get more of these Whales? We're investing all our money in Whales, and those numbers just aren't a good return on investment."

"We don't know if the product is ready for Whales, to be honest with you. We can close mid-market customers quite well, but the big ones, the ones that are million-dollar-a-year clients, we can't seem to crack them and we don't know why. We think it might be the product itself."

"So are you telling me, we've spent this much time going after Whales all year long, and none of you even *believe* we can actually get those kinds of customers in the door? Why haven't you been this honest before?!"

A brief but painful silence fell over the room. "Well, we all *wanted* to go after Whales, and we believed we could get them.

But the data shows something very different and we think it's because the product isn't ready yet to go after those big customers. Our suggestion is reduce our costs on Whale hunting and allocate for Elephant hunting."

It wasn't what we wanted to hear. But it was the indisputable, metric truth.

We learned things—painful, important things.

We came to understand that we had taken too long to make a decision we didn't really want to make. We wanted to believe what the data disputed from the beginning.

Because we wanted the untrue to be true, we siloed our communication and our metrics, separating the real from what we wanted to be real.

As async leaders, we'd done the unthinkable: We put our belief in front of what our team and our data were telling us.

Moreover, our actions were distorted by our *wants,* of course they were. The real reason we hadn't changed course was because we desperately wanted to be Whale hunters instead of training hard to be the best Elephant hunters in the jungle.

Once we had the courage to face the metrics head-on, our real work could finally begin.

21 RULES FOR MANAGING ASYNC REMOTE TEAMS

1. Measure as much as possible automatically in an async way so management can manage without directly interfering with deep work.
2. Implement systems and processes inside of your organization.

3. Forget about showing up on set work hours outside of synchronous meetings (which should be rare) and workers who need to run specific shifts.
4. Track work output and analyze work input but don't get too concerned about managing the process in between. That will figure itself out pretty quickly.
5. Organize a system of overlapping times for communicating in different time zones if you need to do synchronous work.
6. Do a quarterly review of targets, measure those targets weekly with quantitative measures that they can move.
7. Have a chat room open constantly. We have a water cooler chat on Slack.
8. Be wary of chat and email overload. If you're spending more than a day per week on internal email and chat, you're being bothered too much.
9. Use tools for quick video or visual communication. We love Vidyard.
10. When you do synchronous meetings, be as information rich as possible. Video, audio, and a shared screen or whiteboard all allow you to communicate information clearly.
11. Set up a reporting cadence that is ideally automated but regardless must be reported consistently. If your direct reports aren't giving you the numbers you need to confirm the work is moving forward, you're acting blind.
12. Use documents that you can collaborate asynchronously on, like Google Docs.

13. Set up a project management system and actually use it.
14. Test new employees with short-term work before hiring them full time.
15. Look for people who are the right fit for remote async work—egoless, independent, self-starters are the best.
16. Create a standard onboarding process for educating new employees about your company. This is usually inside of your process documents.
17. Inspire leadership through asynchronous ways—videos are a great way to do this. Check out X-Team's videos on YouTube.
18. When you meet synchronously, make it count, talk about the root issues, even if it makes people uncomfortable.
19. Nurture remote friendships. It's totally possible both for you and your team.
20. Beware of a mixed office and remote culture. Remote team members need to have just as much access to information and decision makers as on-premise ones.
21. If you work on-premise, that shouldn't stop you from working asynchronously. Your subordinates will thank you for it.

CHAPTER 8 TAKEAWAYS

1. For many years, technology has been perceived as the enemy of autonomy. The remote pioneers have proved the opposite.
2. By making platforms the office, the async organization is more autonomous than was thought possible.
3. Platforms give all team players the power to participate in their own time and space.
4. Platforms also leave a granular history, helping to broaden knowledge for every team member who wants to get onboard or expand his or her skill set.
5. The first mandate for managing an autonomous team is encouraging team members to demo often, in a totally exposed fashion, for adjustment and course correction.
6. The async manager must focus on EQ, since data points are already exposed to everyone.
7. Too much data can lead to a management decision stasis. In an async environment, choosing something is always preferable to doing nothing.
8. Big freedom can also bring "altitude sickness" to those trained in a permission-first culture; a good async manager helps facilitate the journey toward autonomy.
9. The goal is to cut a path toward imperfect action, executed as cheaply and as quickly as possible.
10. With good processes and metrics in place, every manager should be able to walk away from his or

her department without fear of things going off the rails.

11. There are times when it is necessary to go synchronous with your team. Make it as focused and efficient as possible.
12. Most of all, async managers need to remember that they are not the watchdogs of the old-school office environment. Their job is to facilitate and encourage. Let the platform and the metrics do the rest.

OUTRO

The Future Just Happened

It's our contention that, going forward, every job that can be made remote will be—not because we want it that way, but because it's the endpoint for asynchronous work, an operational technological inevitability. It's cheaper, faster, clearer, and smarter.

What this means for the future of work cannot yet be known, but at the very least, we must accept that the global landscape is changing, very fast. The old office is just that—old—and it's slated for extinction. The remote pioneers may be one of the few groups who've had a full taste of what lies ahead.

On the one hand, countries like Germany, Estonia, Portugal, Costa Rica, Spain, and dozens of others are already setting up remote-friendly policies to help adapt to international business; workers everywhere are more accustomed than ever to "rubbing shoulders" with coworkers from other nations; and new workforces are cropping up all over the planet.

On the other hand, it's likely that we will soon see "labor wars," tariffs, and new limiting policies that curtail international remote work.

Moreover, within each country, a great divide is already developing—the "international" autonomous/asynchronous remote community versus the "local," location-dependent workforce.

The trends we anticipate may sound extreme to newbies, but most remote pioneers agree that the majority of the US workforce will soon be remote for all time. We believe that, by the time we publish this book, the remote revolution will be particularly explosive because the business model will have been proven and the counter-argument will be disproven—by failing organizations, poor employee retention, and plummeting profits. People will have gone back to the office, and many will see that they dislike it, or even more likely, their bosses will see that it's no longer profitable to maintain the office. No matter how much you enjoyed your rotary phone, it just isn't useful in the age of the cell phone. Asynchronous work is that change, and it's moving at lightning speed.

The number of people who live in one country and work for a company in another country is also certain to explode, as the developing world catches up, fueled by Earth-wide, high-speed satellite internet such as Elon Musk's ambitious Starlink system. These satellites replace costly cell phone towers and telephone wire, making way for cheap and instant access. In five years, Africa will likely be unrecognizable from a workforce point of view, with a new competitive edge that challenges both the West and its top outsource allies.

Or, to put it another way: The last two to three billion people who don't have internet access are about to get it. Get ready.

From where we stand, the world and its myriad companies are going remote, without a doubt. Will you be on the winning side or the losing side? That all depends on your willingness to let go of the old ways.

We also contend that these changes—to economy, lifestyle, hiring practices, work terms, and more—can be implemented anywhere. Our hope is that the benefits of asynchronous remote work will become applicable even to location-dependent companies.

In the short term, here are just a few of the implications of the sweeping changes underfoot.

The majority of the companies who have gone remote aren't going back. The August 2021 Job Seeker Survey found that 41 percent of current job holders or job seekers expect to work remotely one day a week or more in the next year. And 19 percent expected to work remotely full-time. Findings from the same survey show that Americans value workplace flexibility (56 percent) more than higher pay (53 percent) and job security (47 percent).

To offer their employees flexible work arrangements, 66 percent of business decision-makers said they were considering transforming their workspaces to accommodate a hybrid workforce. A recent KayoCloud survey confirms the same,[1] finding that 82 percent of individuals with budgetary authority in their businesses envision a hybrid work model.

The Great Resignation leads to the Great Migration. We are currently seeing a huge spike in the number of people who want to leave their jobs. Workers are clearly stating that they want job flexibility above higher pay or job security. They're recognizing that work is no longer a place—it's something you can take with you, wherever you go.

According to the Workforce Pulse Survey by PwC, 45 percent of Gen Z and 47 percent of millennial employees would give up 10 percent or more of their future earnings for an opportunity to work remotely. The Microsoft WTI reports that 46 percent of remote workers plan to relocate. And many already have. A survey conducted by PwC found that 12 percent of employees had moved more than fifty miles from their office location since the pandemic began.

An anonymous worker that we know at one of the largest social media companies in the world makes more than $400,000 a year. He reached out to us at the beginning of the pandemic after he was given the ability to work remotely. He had a simple question: *How much would it cost to get a place in Bali?* The going rate is about US$2,000 a month for a nice three-bedroom villa with a housekeeper. The next month he messaged us from Ubud in Bali telling us that our last phone call had changed his life.

Months later, his company required that employees show up at the office once a month. He didn't mind. He's currently flying halfway across the world once a month for his one day of collaboration. He's also considering moving to the Mexican coast or Costa Rica to shorten the flight. His employer is currently in a state of "don't ask, don't tell," but it won't be long before the cat is out of the bag: It's just a matter of time before the world will not only have to deal with people quitting their jobs due to the pandemic, but also due to the lack of concentration in the labor market. Top-tier talent are becoming digital nomads en masse. They will no longer be set up in one city, state, country, continent, or hemisphere. The sooner you get used it, the better.

Most, if not all, hyper-growth companies will be asynchronous and remote in the near future. The year 1915 was great for horses, there were 26,493,000 of them, the biggest global population of horses in human history. By 1960, their numbers dwindled to about three million. Horses are still a great way to get around today, but we don't see many at the local drive-thru. A decade from now, there will be people who still pine for the good old days when you'd spend hours commuting into a place to spend company time talking about whether Times New Roman or Arial should be on the letterhead, but rest assured, much like those lovable horses, the old office is going extinct. Companies will be running on an Async Mindset, not because they want to or because they think they can or should but because it's inevitable. History teaches us that whenever there is a superior technological change in any aspect of society adoption swiftly follows. It's sometimes painful, and we fully expect challenges for employers and employees alike on this journey, but if you keep your head in the sand, you just might end up headed for the glue factory.

Most middle-manager jobs will cease to exist. Obviously, a bold remark like this scares the crap out of management—that's why they're so resistant to remote work when owners and employees are very much for it. The Async Mindset is, to a large degree, the automation of management. In the future, the role called "manager" will be working on emotional and cultural issues, not micro-demands and management by presence. More of a company's time will be spent *doing* work versus preparing for and overseeing it. If you're reading this and you're a manager, this is your chance to adapt to the new async model of management now so you won't be left behind.

***Not* implementing an asynchronous management model will quickly burn out staff.** Remote workers learned early that using the Async Mindset was the only way to stop the onslaught of video calls that have made current remote work so stressful for a new generation of Zoomers. The early remote pioneers didn't even have video calls—we worked almost exclusively through instant chat, email, and early async project management tools like Basecamp. Give your employees a break and go async. What the majority of the recent converts to remote don't understand—and hopefully we've made it abundantly clear here—is that remote work should not recreate the office. By giving workers the opportunity to work asynchronously, you enable them to embrace deep work and become exponentially more productive than their on-premise counterparts. This makes for happier, healthier workers. Without the clear targets, the lack of distractions, and the clear documentation that the Async Mindset demands, truly deep work is not possible.

Information communication technology will empower employers and employees to find the best of one another. When we look at communication networks like the Starlink satellite internet network or the rise of the metaverse for online collaboration, we see that technology itself is empowering proof of work as the measurement of success. This means that where you're from or who you know just doesn't matter as much anymore. Good riddance to all that!

Discrimination will further erode under an Async Mindset. The remote pioneers don't care what you look like, who you pray to, or who you vote for. We care if you get your work done and you treat other team members with the same respect we provide you. By making a meritocracy possible, we are also giving anyone access to meaningful, profitable, rewarding work. That's something worth defending.

Economic barriers will collapse in the upcoming remote world. In a way, they already have. We remember having to book an office in Las Vegas because no merchant account would do business with us without one. That office still exists, we've been in it once, and it's depressing as hell.

When we think of what we needed to do to be "legit" back then, compared to the way things are now, it's laughable. Platforms like Wise.com are already allowing anyone to send anyone else money at lower and lower costs. Cryptocurrency platforms like the remote-first Coinbase will allow commerce to exist outside national frameworks, creating an environment where anyone, anywhere, can do business with anyone else, with a few clicks of a mouse. These platforms don't exist under a single power structure, and they will continue to erode nation-state control over commerce at greater and more stupendous scales.

It is our deep hope that the lessons of the remote pioneers will permeate not just our culture but the whole world, allowing for a fairer, happier meritocracy.

For example, take the unofficial poster boy for Running Remote, Fahim Karim. His life illustrates exactly what we mean when we say that going remote makes all workers truly equal.

Over a period of several months, young Fahim of Bangladesh cobbled enough money together to buy a laptop and train himself to be a graphics designer. By 2020, he had more than five hundred five-star ratings for his work and was one of the most popular designers on the popular remote worksite Fiverr.

All this, and no one was aware that he had muscular dystrophy and could only move one hand. Fahim made it a point to never interact with anyone via video—he didn't want to bias clients. Ultimately, Fahim's physical challenges didn't stop him from becoming one of the top-ranked designers in the world.

When we think about challenges in our own lives, it pains us to realize that Fahim would probably trade his best day for our worst and, yet, only in a remote/async context would somebody like him be able to be not merely useful, but excellent.

If it wasn't for remote work, Fahim would likely have ended up panhandling in the streets of Bangladesh. Instead, he found a place in the global economy, a home. Moreover, Fahim didn't just become a worker or a staff member—he became a full-fledged async entrepreneur.

In fall 2020, we lost so much, including Fahim.

Still, Fahim's life remains a shining example of what remote async work promises for the world. Async gave Fahim the power to have a meaningful life.

Your work is what's important—not where you're from, who you know, or what others think you are capable of. Life is too short to build your company in a cubicle, offering your staff stale jelly beans that they'll hate anyway as you force them to work on things they don't care about.

In Fahim's wake, a whole planet is making itself ready to let go of bias, to judge by skill and talent alone. The Async Mindset kicks open this door for so many—people who no longer want to settle for mere survival because of where they are or who they are.

Like Fahim, you can be a true remote pioneer.

NOTES

Intro

1. Iva Marinova, "28 Need-to-Know Remote Work Statistics of 2021," Review 42, January 4, 2022, https://review42.com/resources/remote-work-statistics/.

Chapter 1

1. Hanna Mansson, "The History of the Office: Office Trends through the Centuries," *Hubble*, August 20, 2021, https://hubblehq.com/blog/the-history-of-the-office.
2. Jill Lepore, "Burnout: Modern Affliction or Human Condition?" *The New Yorker*, May 24, 2021, https://www.newyorker.com/magazine/2021/05/24/burnout-modern-affliction-or-human-condition?source=search_google_dsa_paid&gclid=CjwKCAiA55mPBhBOEiwANmzoQo84E7sXhjENE_NhlQYthjDuAg_mUMxu9jedPg4vSHOlH_mp6m6UgBoCt8wQAvD_BwE.
3. Marshall McLuhan, Quentin Fiore, Jerome Agel, *The Medium Is the Massage: An Inventory of Effects* (Berkeley, Calif.: Gingko Press, 2001), pp. 74–75.
4. Carlos, "63 Surprising Digital Nomad Statistics in 2021," A Brother Abroad, January 3, 2022, https://abrotherabroad.com/digital-nomad-statistics/.

5. Jon Younger, "The Best Destinations For Digital Nomads: A New Survey," *Forbes*, May 24, 2021, https://www.countries4me.com/the-best-destinations-for-digital-nomads-a-new-survey/.

Chapter 2

1. Interview with Amir Salihefendić.

Chapter 3

1. Merit Morikawa, "16 Examples of Open Innovation—What Can We Learn from Them?" Viima, November 20, 2016, https://www.viima.com/blog/16-examples-of-open-innovation-what-can-we-learn-from-them.

Chapter 4

1. Isaac Kohen, "Productivity Metrics Matter More Than Ever for SMBs: How to Measure Your Workforce Effectively in 2021," business.com, November 10, 2020, https://www.business.com/articles/productivity-metrics-remote-workers/.
2. Kenjo, "How to Use KPIs for Measuring Remote Productivity," Kenjo blog, 2022, https://blog.kenjo.io/how-to-use-kpis-for-measuring-remote-productivity.

Chapter 5

1. Mathew J. Wedel, "A Monument of Inefficiency: The Presumed Course of the Recurrent Laryngeal Nerve in Sauropod Dinosaurs," BioOne Complete, May 20, 2011, https://bioone.org/journals/acta-palaeontologica-polonica/volume-57/issue-2/app.2011.0019/A-Monument-of-Inefficiency–The-Presumed-Course-of-the/10.4202/app.2011.0019.full#:~:text=The%20recurrent%20laryngeal%20nerve%20is,the%20development%20of%20the%20neck.

2. Emily Courtney, "Remote Work Statistics: Navigating the New Normal," FlexJobs, https://www.flexjobs.com/blog/post/remote-work-statistics/.
3. Enda Curran, "Work from Home to Lift Productivity by 5% in Post-Pandemic U.S.," Bloomberg, April 22, 2021, https://www.bloomberg.com/news/articles/2021-04-22/yes-working-from-home-makes-you-more-productive-study-finds.
4. Katharine Swindell, "People—and Jobs—Are Fleeing the Bay Area. Is This the End of Silicon Valley?" Techmonitor, March 2, 2021, https://techmonitor.ai/leadership/workforce/people-jobs-fleeing-bay-area-is-this-end-of-silicon-valley.
5. Aytekin Tank, "Why the World Fell Out of Love with Silicon Valley," Jotform, December 20, 2019, https://www.jotform.com/blog/silicon-valley-today/.
6. "Big Tech Changes Tack on US Privacy Regulation," *Financial Times*, https://www.ft.com/content/767a24bc-c637-11e8-ba8f-ee390057b8c9.
7. Maya Kosoff, "The Next Big Anti-tech Backlash Is Just Beginning," *Vanity Fair*, May 29, 2018, https://www.vanityfair.com/news/2018/05/the-next-big-anti-tech-backlash-is-just-beginning.
8. Olivia Solon, "Scraping by on Six Figures? Tech Workers Feel Poor in Silicon Valley's Wealth Bubble," *The Guardian*, February 27, 2017, https://www.theguardian.com/technology/2017/feb/27/silicon-aa-cost-of-living-crisis-has-americas-highest-paid-feeling-poor.
9. Jay Rao, "What Silicon Valley Gets Wrong (and Right) About Culture," Quartz at Work, April 24, 2018, https://qz.com/work/1260607/what-silicon-valley-gets-wrong-and-right-about-culture/.
10. Job van der Voort, *Global Workforce Revolution Report*, 2020, Remote, https://f.hubspotusercontent00.net/hubfs/7405301/Global-Workforce-Revolution-Report.pdf.
11. Rebecca Stropoli, "Are We Really More Productive Working from Home?" *Chicago Booth Review*, August 18, 2021, https://

www.chicagobooth.edu/review/are-we-really-more-productive-working-home.

12. Edward Glaeser and David Cutler, "You May Get More Work Done at Home. But You'd Have Better Ideas at the Office," *The Washington Post*, September 24, 2021, https://www.washingtonpost.com/outlook/2021/09/24/working-home-productivity-pandemic-remote/.

Chapter 6

1. Estelle Pin, "Our New Study Takes a Deeper Look into the State of Remote Work," TINYpulse, February 23, 2018, https://www.tinypulse.com/blog/the-state-of-remote-work.
2. Iva Marinova, "28 Need-to-Know Remote Work Statistics of 2022," Review 42, January 17, 2022, https://review42.com/resources/remote-work-statistics/.
3. Owl Labs, *State of Remote Work*, 2020, https://owllabs.com/state-of-remote-work/2020.
4. Lori Ioannou, "Vast Migration of Over 14 Million Americans Coming Due to Rise in Remote Work, Study Shows," CNBC, October 29, 2020, https://www.cnbc.com/2020/10/28/vast-migration-of-over-14-million-americans-coming-due-to-remote-work.html.
5. Chase Warrington, "How to Build Human Connections in an Async Workplace," Doist Blog, https://blog.doist.com/humanizing-async-work/.

Chapter 7

1. Joey Hadden, Lara Casado, Tyler Sonnemaker, and Taylor Borden, "17 Major Companies That Have Announced Employees Can Work Remotely Long Term," *Entrepreneur*, August 17, 2020 (reprinted from *Business Insider*), https://www.entrepreneur.com/article/354872.

Chapter 8

1. "US Employee 'Outsourced Job to China,'" BBC News, January 16, 2013, https://www.bbc.com/news/technology-21043693.

Outro

1. "11 Shocking Statistics on the Great Resignation," Ergonomic Trends, November 4, 2021, https://ergonomictrends.com/great-resignation-statistics/.

ABOUT THE AUTHORS

LIAM AND ROB are cofounders of the Running Remote conference and community and have built multiple remote businesses, including Time Doctor, a global business with more than 130 team members in thirty countries. They have worked together for more than a decade despite living on opposite sides of the planet.

They now speak at conferences around the world, including SXSW, SaaS Stock, Nomad City, HR of Tomorrow, and The Digital Workplace, and have consulted with more remote-first founders and operators than probably anyone else in the asynchronous space today.

Learn more and contact them at RunningRemoteBook.com.

PUT ASYNC INTO PRACTICE

Had enough theory and ready to make working remote work for you and your team?

Find free resources to help right now at **runningremotebook.com**

Share your progress, sticking points, and wins with **#runningremotebook**

THINK ASYNC!